British
Locomotive Names
of the
Twentieth Century

by

H. C. Casserley

LONDON

IAN ALLAN

A36184

6 25. 26

11. 10. 67

Printed and bound in the United Kingdom by
STAPLES PRINTERS LIMITED
at their Stratford, London, establishment

Contents

Preface to Second Edition

This revised edition has been brought up to date to include additional names and other information which have accrued since the original publication, which appeared in 1963, together with eight additional pages of photographs.

Actual new names are not numerous, being mainly confined to sundry British Railways main line diesel locomotives, and in which connection it seems somewhat extraordinary that it has not so far been seen fit to bestow the distinction of a name on any of the new two hundred electric locomotives working much publicised new services between London and Manchester and Liverpool. These engines must now rank as by far the most important and advanced stage in railway traction in the country. If and when it is decided to grace these very deserving machines with something better than a particularly uninteresting series of numbers, surely no better choice could be than a revival of many of the romantic sounding names of the past formerly to be found on the L.N.W.R. engines which used to work the same trains, the 'Jumbos' and the 'Precursors' in particular.

For various corrections and amendments in the main section I am indebted to Mr E. F. Hodges and other correspondents, whilst for much additional information in the chapter devoted to the railways of Ireland I must thank Mr R. F. Clements, well known expert on locomotive matters across the Irish Sea.

H. C. Casserley,
Berkhamsted.
January 1967.

Foreword

The practice of naming locomotives dates back to the earliest days of the steam engine. It probably originated from the stage coach, which was at that period in its heyday and relied solely on names as the only means of identification of the many hundreds in use on the roads of Great Britain at the time. Ships have also for several centuries been distinguished by their names, a practice which continues to this day. But the idea has never been applied to aircraft, to distinguish individual machines of the same design from one another.

It is curious that the practice of giving names to locomotives has been so much more widespread in the British Isles than elsewhere on overseas railways, where a named locomotive, especially in more recent times, but also in the past, seems to have been a distinct rarity in most foreign countries.

Of all the well-known names applied to the earliest steam locomotives, Stephenson's 'Rocket' was probably the most famous of them all, and may still be regarded almost as a household word, frequently met with in common usage as referring to any steam engine, modern or otherwise, but now regarded as old-fashioned or out of date. Locomotive students will, of course, be familiar with many of the lesser-known pioneers of the steam locomotive: 'Novelty,' 'Sanspareil,' 'Northumbrian,' 'Invicta,' and all the rest of that gallant band, but it is perhaps significant of the later trend in locomotive identification that even the famous 'Locomotion' of 1825, often but erroneously regarded as the first steam locomotive ever to run, bore in addition to its name also the distinctive 'No. 1.' Subsequent engines built for the Stockton and Darlington Railway were likewise distinguished by numbers in addition to their names. No. 2 'Hope,' No. 3 'Black Diamond,' No. 4 'Diligence,' and so on. As other railways came into existence during the initial expansion period of the 1830's and 1840's the practice of identification varied between one concern and another, and although most of the many varied types of locomotives which appeared were given some form of appellation the practice tended to die out on some of the newly-formed companies created by the amalgamation of former ones. By the time the major railways were established in the form in which they were to remain in most cases right down to the grouping of 1923 there had become definite divergences in practice in this respect. Of the principal Companies only two, the Great Western and the London and North Western, adopted the policy of consistently naming all of their express passenger locomotives practically throughout the whole period of their existence, although the L.N.W.R. dropped it almost, but not entirely, towards the end, largely as an economy measure during the first world war. Even on these two lines, the idea of applying names to freight and tank engines had long since been abandoned, except in the case of the G.W.R. broad gauge, of which a certain proportion of the locomotives were never numbered, and continued throughout their career to be known by their names alone. Best known among these were the famous Brunel 4-2-2's, which right up to their demise in 1892, when the broad gauge was finally abandoned, were never numbered in the locomotive stock. These engines were almost unique in this respect throughout the British Isles, the only parallel in modern times, so far as a public railway is concerned, being found in the small Sligo Leitrim and Northern Counties Railway in Ireland, which maintained its independence right up to its enforced closure in 1957, and whose small fleet of locomotives were distinguished by names alone right to the end.

Of the other major companies, the Midland, the Great Northern and Great Eastern stand out as adopting the most consistent anti-naming policy and each of these great railways managed to name but two engines apiece during the whole of their independent existence. The North Eastern, as successors to the Stockton and Darlington, which as previously mentioned, applied the number 1 in addition to the name to its very first locomotive, likewise abandoned the practice at a very early date, and only revived it at the close of its existence with its five Pacifics constructed in 1922. The Lancashire and Yorkshire was another line which in its later days possessed no named locomotives apart from its small narrow gauge shunters at Horwich works, and in a similar category came the London and South Western, on which line the naming of engines generally ceased after Mr Adams came on the scene in 1878, although here an exception was made in the case of the 0-4-0T's built for use in Southampton Docks, and there were also a few other miscellaneous engines of the same wheel arrangement acquired from outside sources.

The London, Brighton and South Coast, on the other hand, under Stroudley's regime, consistently named all of its engines (tanks included), apart from its 0-6-0 goods engines, but most regrettably these were nearly all removed by Mr Marsh from 1905 onwards, although they were retained in a few cases right up to the grouping. Of the other southern companies, the London, Chatham and Dover had a few named engines at the time of the amalgamation of 1899 into the South Eastern and Chatham, but the other partner, the South Eastern, had practically none, and thereafter the newly formed S.E. & C.R. eschewed the practice entirely.

The Manchester, Sheffield and Lincolnshire, which became the Great Central in 1900, had not gone in for naming for many years, but the newly formed G.C.R. made a spasmodic attempt with a few odd engines in its earlier years and somewhat more consistently in its last days.

Amongst the Scottish lines, the Highland was the most consistent in adopting a naming policy, which it applied to most of its passenger engines, including a few tanks, but of the remainder, the Caledonian gave names to only a few selected engines, as did the North British in its earlier years, but this Company in latter days named all of its principal passenger locomotives. The Great North of Scotland bestowed names on only its final series of 4-4-0 engines, and the Glasgow and South Western on only one.

Of the Irish lines, the locomotives, both passenger and freight, of the Great Northern and the Midland Great Western Railway practically all bore names during the early part of the century, but these were in most cases removed during the first world war, and in the case of the M.G.W.R. on its absorption into the G.S.R. in 1925, although the practice was revived on the G.N.R. to some extent in its later years. The Great Southern and Western and the Belfast and Northern Counties each only possessed a few odd locomotives which were honoured in this respect.

It was after the grouping of 1923 that the gradually dying practice—the G.W.R. apart—of naming locomotives, was revived to such an extent, as all four of the newly constituted Companies, the L.M.S.R., L.N.E.R., G.W.R., and S.R. embarked on a definite policy of naming their newly constructed express passenger engines, and in a few cases of applying names to some of the older locomotives already in existence. This practice was continued to a limited extent by British Railways after nationalisation in 1948, but seemed once more to be falling into disfavour when the first express diesels began to appear. Possibly it was felt that there was little point in bestowing high sounding names on these soulless machines lacking the glamour of the steam locomotive, but here again there seems to have been some change of opinion and certain of the latest classes of diesel engines are once again receiving the distinction.

There is, of course, an immense range of variety in the choice of a name; so many fields open themselves, and almost all of them have been brought into use at some time or another, many of them several times over. Broadly speaking, they may be divided under several headings, the more obvious ones being personalities, place-names, historical, and others, each with several sub-divisions. The first category included Kings and Queens, etc., of which there have been very many indeed: historical characters, and so on, but curiously enough musicians have been almost entirely neglected, although poets have also figured to a considerable extent. The G.W.R., it is true, have a 'Sir Edward Elgar,' but almost inexplicably there has never been a Beethoven, Wagner, Mendelssohn, Richard Strauss, or any other of the great figures of musical history. One would have thought, too, that some of the great explorers would have made most suitable names for a series of locomotives, but this is an idea which has never occurred to those responsible for their selection. Place-names probably offer the largest scope of all, countries, cities, counties, all of which have been used several times over, down to the smallest towns and villages served by the railway concerned, a system much favoured by the old L.B. & S.C.R. in particular. The stately homes of England have also received a good deal of attention from the G.W.R., its long series of Halls and also its Manors and Granges being well known. The idea of bestowing names of a common origin to a particular class can be traced back to the early days of the G.W. with its 'Star' series of 2-2-2's, built between 1837 and 1841 (see page 12). It appeared again on the Highland in the 1890's, and was revived by Churchward on the G.W.R. from 1906 onwards with its 'Ladies' and 'Saints,' 'Stars' and so on. Collett carried on the tradition with his numerous 'Halls' and other well-known types.

The final class to which this method was applied, however, the well known 'Castles', was not so consistently followed, as a number of these engines were named, or in some cases renamed, with names of an entirely different origin. After the grouping a similar plan of class naming was adopted by the Southern with its 'King Arthurs', 'Lord Nelsons', and 'Schools'.

Amongst the immense range and variety of names which have graced our locomotives at various times there have been very many which have done much to add to the dignity and grace of man's finest invention, the steam locomotive, but it cannot be denied that in other instances there have been many which must be regarded at least as inappropriate, and in some cases plainly ridiculous. In the latter category must surely be placed the series of G.W.R. 4-4-0's which were christened by the names of flowers, 'Carnation', 'Primrose' etc., which however pleasant sounding in their own sphere seem a misnomer when applied to a locomotive. The L.N.E.R.'s idea of naming some of its Pacifics after racehorses, too, whilst excellent in itself, had somewhat unfortunate results in practice when these fine machines were observed bearing such appellations as 'Sandwich', 'Spearmint', 'Pretty Polly', and 'Blink Bonny'.

Fashions have changed much over the years, and many of the names which appeared on our early locomotives would be hardly acceptable to-day, and might be greeted with a certain degree of caustic comment or ribaldry, for instance 'Liver', 'Sisyphus' (L.N.W.R.) and 'Pollux' (G.W.R.). There has recently however been a slight tendency to revive some of these old and somewhat obscure names in the B.R. Deltic diesels. The general tendency nowadays is to utilise more mundane and specialised names: regiments, for instance on the L.M.S. 'Royal Scots', and numbers of R.A.F. Squadrons as applied to the 'Battle of Britain' series of S.R. Pacifics.

The most common position for displaying the name on a locomotive is on the driving wheel splashers, or in the case of a tank engine, in the most obvious place on the tank side. The modern tendency for the running plate to become even higher, however, and the splasher progressively smaller, in many more recent designs disappearing altogether, has resulted in a new position having to be found, sometimes a plate placed over the central driving wheel, or on the side of the boiler barrel, whilst in some later types advantage has been taken of the comparatively modern steam deflectors placed at the sides of the smokebox. The plate on the boiler barrel was however not uncommonly used on earlier designs, such as those on the Great Northern of Ireland.

In early days the name usually took the form of a brass plate with raised lettering of handsome design, which persisted in the case of the Great Western right to the end of its independent existence, but the general tendency in later years was for plates to assume a plainer pattern, usually of cast iron, and recently even aluminium has come into use. Some early engines on the Great Western and other railways had names composed of individual brass letters attached to the framing or some other part of the locomotive.

In many cases, however, on lines such as the Brighton and the Highland, plates were never used, the names being hand painted in varying styles. With this method there was a somewhat increased danger of an engine losing its name altogether when going through the works for a complete overhaul. It also made renaming a rather simpler process, as occurred so much on the Highland.

Of recent years, owing to the regrettable activities of souvenir hunters, British Railways have found it necessary to remove the nameplates from their remaining steam locomotives, with the result that very few of the last survivors have carried their names to the end, although in a few cases wooden replicas have been provided, or the names hand-painted.

It would not be practicable, however, even if the required information was completely available, to record in this book every name which has been borne by a locomotive in the British Isles since early days, but taking, roughly speaking, the turn of the century as a starting point, it has been attempted to consider each railway in turn and detail the names which have been borne by that Company's engines from about the year 1900 onwards, down to the present time, 1967.

An exception has been made in the case of the famous Gooch single wheelers of the Great Western, as although the broad gauge was abolished in 1892, it is felt that any history of named engines would be incomplete without including these well known locomotives of a former decade.

The method of presentation is such that the book is divided into seven parts.

The first comprises the Great Western together with all of its associated and absorbed railways and the next three take all of the lines which came respectively into the London Midland and Scottish, London and North Eastern, and Southern Railways, at the grouping in 1923, together with any new engines built to these Companies' designs thereafter until Nationalisation in 1948.

Part five deals with the British Railways Standard designs, steam, electric and diesel, section six is devoted to the Irish Railways, whilst the final section seven covers all the independent lines not coming within any of the previous categories, including a few industrial concerns. It would not be practicable to detail all of the many hundreds of such locomotives, if only for reasons of space, but a small selection is included of engines in this category of particular interest especially from a naming point of view.

Many instances occur of renaming, and in these cases successive names borne by an engine are indicated by means of an oblique line between the two or more names carried at various times during an engine's lifetime.

All photographs are by the author, except where otherwise stated, and in one or two instances where the authorship is unknown.

1
Great Western Railway

From the 1890's until the end of its existence as an individual railway, the Great Western carried out a consistent policy of naming all its express passenger engines, and along with the London and North Western, which had adopted the practice from an even earlier period, they stand out as the two railways in the British Isles, and doubtless anywhere in the world, which during their existence had possessed by far the greatest number of named engines.

The Great Western standard style of nameplate, which originated as long ago as 1846 on a broad gauge 2-2-2 turned out from Swindon in that year, was a particularly handsome thing. Curved in shape to follow the contour of the driving wheel splasher, it consisted of a heavy brass sector with a pleasing style of raised lettering, distinctive in appearance and very easily legible even at a considerable distance when kept clean, as it always was until the second world war. The exact style of lettering and format varied slightly through the years, but the general appearance remained in effect constant for just over a century.

For a few years between 1894 and 1901 two other styles of name display were experimented with on some series of engines of the 'Duke of Cornwall', 'Bulldog' and 'Badminton' class 4-4-0's, the first consisting of a rectangular nameplate on the side of the smokebox, or boiler, and even in some cases the firebox, and the second a large oval brass plate on the cabside bearing number, name, and constructional details, and these composite nameplates lasted in most cases throughout the engines' existence.

Generally speaking, however, the curved design was adhered to right to the end with a few exceptions to which the shape was not suitable, notably with sundry tank engines which bore names and with Hawksworth's 'County' class 4-6-0's of 1945, to which it could not conveniently be applied, and where a rectangular shape had to be adopted.

It is interesting to observe that the original 2-2-2 of 1846, the first engine built at Swindon, bore the name 'Great Western', which appellation was fittingly applied to one of the last engines to be built at Swindon under G.W.R. auspices, 'Castle' class No. 7007, which was turned out in 1946, at first as 'Ogmore Castle', but renamed 'Great Western' in commemoration when the Company finally lost its identity under Nationalisation in January 1948. Another thirty of these fine engines were to appear during the next three years under the new regime, and the last of these, No. 7037, was again most appropriately named 'Swindon'.

This handsome style of nameplate was perpetuated – although in its rectangular form – by Swindon with its first main line diesel engines of the

11

'Warship' class, but in the later 'Western' series, the lettering has degenerated to a simpler and less ornate style, more in keeping with modern tendencies.

BROAD GAUGE SINGLE WHEELERS

As the 7' 0" gauge on the Great Western was abolished in 1892, the broad gauge engines cannot of course be included in any record of the present century, which is the period which this volume aims in general to cover. It is felt, however, that an exception should be made in the case of the famous Gooch single wheelers constructed from 1847 onwards by both Gooch and Armstrong, and which remained the principal type of express engines until the final abolition of the broad gauge.

They were always known only by their names, and were never numbered, the complete list in order of construction being as follows:

*Iron Duke	Rougemont	*Balaklava
*Great Britain	*Hirondelle	*Inkermann
*Lightning	*Tornado	Kertch
*Emperor	*Prometheus	*Crimea
Pasha	Perseus	*Eupatoria
*Sultan	Estafette	*Sebastopol
*Courier	*Rover	*Swallow
*Tartar	*Amazon	Timour
*Dragon	Lord of the Isles	Bulkeley
*Warlock	*Alma	Great Western
Wizard		

In the case of those marked with an asterisk there were actually two engines bearing these names, the original being scrapped in the 1870's and replaced by new machines of practically identical design. Construction of the type continued fairly evenly over a long period, on an average of about three or four engines a year between 1847 and 1855, and again from 1871 to 1880, whilst a final three, 'Great Western', and the second 'Prometheus' and 'Tornado', as late as 1888. As the gauge was abolished in 1892, these last three had a very short working life.

Before leaving the broad gauge, mention should be made also of the earlier 'Star' class 2-2-2's, built between 1837 and 1841, a series of twelve engines bearing names identical with those which were revived many years later by Churchward on his original 4 cylinder engines built in 1906/7, Nos. 4000–4010, with an additional name, 'Bright Star', which did not reappear. Of the old 2-2-2's the most famous of them all was the original engine 'North Star', which on withdrawal in 1871 was preserved in Swindon works until 1906, when it was most regrettably broken up. A life size replica of the engine as originally constructed was made in 1925 for the Darlington Centenary celebrations, and this is still in existence.

At the turn of the century, the principal class of express engines at work on the G.W.R. was a very fine series of 4-2-2 engines with outside frames, numbered 3001–3080.

The first thirty had been built in 1891 and 1892 as 2-2-2 engines, and Nos. 3021–3028 were actually turned out with the wheels outside the frames for the 7′ 0″ broad gauge and ran in this form during the last months of its existence, after which they were converted to the standard gauge. All of the 2-2-2 engines were rebuilt as 4-2-2's in 1894, and Nos. 3031–3080, built new to this design, were turned out between 1894 and 1899.

After a few years of express duties these single wheelers were gradually ousted by 4 and 6 wheel coupled types, and they were taken out of service between 1908 and 1915. A certain amount of renaming occurred with some of the engines, as shown in the accompanying table, and in a few other cases were latterly removed altogether owing to duplication caused by newer engines having received the same names.

Later Number	*Name*	*Later Number*	*Name*
3001	Amazon	3035	Bellerophon/Beaufort
3002	Atalanta	3036	Crusader
3003	Avalanche	3037	Corsair
3004	Black Prince	3038	Devonia
3005	Britannia	3039	Dreadnought
3006	Courier	3040	Empress of India
3007	Dragon	3041	Emlyn/The Queen/
3008	Emperor		James Mason
3009	Flying Dutchman	3042	Frederick Saunders
3010	Fire King	3043	Hercules
3011	Greyhound	3044	Hurricane
3012	Great Western	3045	Hirondelle
3013	Great Britain	3046	Lord of the Isles
3014	Iron Duke	3047	Lorna Doone
3015	Kennet	3048	Majestic
3016	Lightning	3049	Prometheus/Nelson
3017	Nelson/Prometheus	3050	Royal Sovereign
3018	Racer/Glenside	3051	Stormy Petrel
3019	Rover	3052	Sir Walter Raleigh
3020	Sultan	3053	Sir Francis Drake
3021	Wigmore Castle	3054	Sir Richard Grenville
3022	Rougemont/Bessemer	3055	Trafalgar/Lambert
3023	Swallow	3056	Timour/Wilkinson
3024	Storm King	3057	Tartar/Walter Robinson
3025	St. George/Quicksilver	3058	Ulysses/Grierson
3026	Tornado	3059	Voltigeur/John W. Wilson
3027	Thames/Worcester	3060	Warlock/John G. Griffiths
3028	Wellington	3061	Alexandra/George A. Wills
3029	White Horse	3062	Albert Edward
3030	Westward Ho	3063	Duke of York
3031	Achilles	3064	Duke of Edinburgh
3032	Agamemnon	3065	Duke of Connaught
3033	Albatross	3066	Duchess of Albany
3034	Behemoth	3067	Duchess of Teck

Later		*Later*	
Number	*Name*	*Number*	*Name*
3068	Duke of Cambridge	3075	Princess Louise
3069	Earl of Chester	3076	Princess Beatrice
3070	Earl of Warwick	3077	Princess May
3071	Emlyn	3078	Shooting Star/Eupatoria
3072	North Star/Bulkeley	3079	Thunderbolt
3073	Princess Royal	3080	Windsor Castle
3074	Princess Helena		

Concurrently with the appearance of the Dean 4-2-2's listed above and the various 4-4-0 types shortly to be enumerated, the bulk of the express and ordinary passenger trains on the standard gauge lines of the G.W.R. were in the hands of many and varied series of 2-2-2 and 2-4-0 engines, only a few of which, however, ever bore names. These may be summarised as follows:—

2-2-2 engines with outside frames, built 1873–1875 and mostly withdrawn in the early years of the century.

55	Queen	1119	Prince of Wales
999	Sir Alexander	1122	Beaconsfield
1118	Prince Christian	1130	Gooch

Some earlier 2-2-2 engines, also with outside frames, built 1866-1869

378	Sir Daniel	withdrawn 1898
380	North Star	converted 1902 to 0-6-0 engine (name removed)
381	Morning Star	,, ,, ,,
471	Sir Watkin	converted 1901, etc.

Two 2-2-2 engines, built in 1884 and 1886

| 9 | Victoria | withdrawn 1905 |
| 10 | Royal Albert | ,,   1906 |

2-4-0   Built 1878,   one of a class of eight engines, the only one to receive a name.

154   Chancellor   withdrawn 1919

2-4-0 engines, originally built in 1855–6 as 2-2-2's, but rebuilt in 1895–7 as 2-4-0's. Withdrawn between 1907 and 1918.

| 69 | Avon | 70 | Dart | 71 | Dee | 72 | Exe |
| 73 | Isis | 74 | Stour | 75 | Teign | 76 | Wye |

2-4-0   Built 1884   3201   Stella

This engine had a curious history, as it was sold almost immediately after construction to the Pembroke and Tenby Railway, becoming their No. 8. When this line was absorbed by the G.W.R. in 1896, it received its original number, 3201, and was named "Stella." It lasted until 1933, but had by then lost its name for a considerable time.

4-4-0's 'DUKE OF CORNWALL' AND 'BULLDOG' CLASSES

The history of the 'Duke of Cornwall' and the earlier 'Bulldogs' is somewhat interwoven, as of the original sixty engines, turned out between 1895 and 1899, as Nos. 3252–3291 and 3312–3331, twenty later became the larger 'Bulldog' class, and all except the original engine were renumbered to form two blocks each of one series. For the purposes of this record the engines can best be enumerated as they were after this transformation.

DUKE OF CORNWALL CLASS

Later Number	Renumbered 1946	Name
3252		Duke of Cornwall
3253		Boscawen
3254	9054	Cornubia
3255		Excalibur
3256		Guinevere
3257		King Arthur
3258		Lizard The Lizard
3259		Merlin
3260		Mount Edgecumbe
3261		St. Germans
3262		St. Ives
3263		St. Michael
3264	9064	Trevithick
3265	9065	Tre Pol and Pen
3266		Amyas
3267		Cornishman
3268		Chough
3269		Dartmoor
3270		Earl of Devon
3271		Eddystone
3272	9072	Fowey
3273	9073	Mounts Bay
3274		Newquay
3275		St. Erth
3276	9076	St. Agnes
3277		Tresco/Isle of Tresco
3278		Trefusis
3279		Tor Bay
3280		Tregenna
3281		Cotswold
3282		Chepstow Castle
3283	9083	Comet
3284	9084	Jersey/Isle of Jersey
3285		Katerfelto
3286		Meteor
3287	9087	Mercury
3288		Mendip

Later Number	*Renumbered 1946*	*Name*
3289	9089	St. Austell
3290		Severn
3291	9091	Thames

A number of these engines latterly lost their names, either as a result of construction of new locomotives to which was desired given the same name, or because these being place names were occasionally misconstrued by simple and inexperienced travellers as being destination boards!

Most of the class disappeared prior to 1946, but as shown in the above table eleven of them were renumbered in that year into the 9000's, and the last of these, No. 9054 'Cornubia', survived until 1950.

Parts of twenty nine others were used in 1936–1939 in conjuction with the frames of a corresponding number of 'Bulldogs' for the construction of what virtually amounted to new engines, of which the first thirteen only carried names for a short time, after which these were transferred to new 4-6-0's of the Castle class:—

They were built as follows:—

3200	Earl of Mount Edgcumbe	3207	Earl of St. Germans
3201	Earl of Dunraven	3208	Earl Bathurst
3202	Earl of Dudley	3209	Earl of Radnor
3203	Earl Cawdor	3210	Earl Cairns
3204	Earl of Dartmouth	3211	Earl of Ducie
3205	Earl of Devon	3212	Earl of Eldon
3206	Earl of Plymouth		

These engines became Nos. 9000-9012 in 1946 and were scrapped between 1948 and 1960.

4-4-0's BULLDOG CLASS

As stated in the previous section, the first 'Bulldogs' originated from the 'Duke of Cornwall' class, but with subsequent additions the whole series became more or less standardised, with some detailed and constructional differences, and known generally as the 'Bulldog' class. The principal variation lay in the provision of straight frames from engine 3341 onwards, and eventually all of the engines received standard coned boilers, etc. For some reason a few of the later engines between 3419 and 3440 never received names, and are consequently not included in the following list.

Later Number	*Name*	*Later Number*	*Name*
3300	Pendennis Castle	3306	Armorel
3301	Powderham	3307	Exmoor
3302	Sir Lancelot	3308	Falmouth
3303	St. Anthony	3309	Maristowe/Maristow
3304	Tamar/River Tamar	3310	St. Just
3305	Tintagel	3311	Bulldog

G.W.R. Broad gauge locomotive 'Bulkeley'.

G.W.R. Single wheeler 'The Queen'

An early G.W.R. 4-4-0 No. 3312 (later 3311) 'Bulldog' with the nameplate in
an unusual position on the firebox.

G.W.R. Combined name and numberplate.

G.W.R.—Another type of combined name and numberplate used on certain 4-4-0s.

G.W.R. The original 4-cylinder Atlantic (later converted to 4-6-0.)

G.W.R. 'Saint' class 2-cylinder 4-6-0.

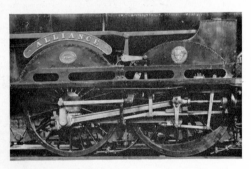

G.W.R. nameplate of French compound No. 104.

G.W.R. nameplate of No. 4932 showing final form of G.W.R. plate, with thicker lettering than in the earlier version.

G.W.R. Its only Pacific, No. 111 'The Great Bear'.

G.W.R. The last of the Castles, No. 7037, appropriately named 'Swindon'.

G.W.R.—'Lady Margaret', formerly a Liskeard and Looe engine.

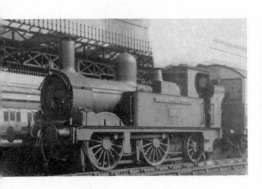

G.W.R.—'Fair Rosamund'. Another of the few named tank engines.

G.W.R.—'Margaret' a small saddle tank acquired from the Gwendraeth Valley Railway.

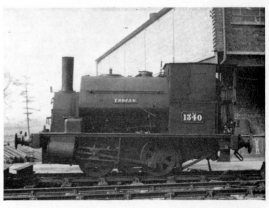

Nameplate of Vale of Rheidol section engine No. 7.

G.W.R.—No. 1340 'Trojan', formerly Alexandra (Newport & South Wales) Docks & Railway, still running in 1966 at Alders Paper Mills.

Mawddwy Railway 0-6-0ST, later taken over by the Cambrian, and eventually G.W.R. No. 824.

[E. H. Seward

'Fox', a 0-4-0ST of 1872 acquired from the West Cornwall Railway.

[L.P.C

Former Brecon and Merthyr engine sold to Cyfarthfa Ironworks as 'Cyfarthfa 12'.

Later Number	Name	Later Number	Name
3312	Guernsey/Isle of Guernsey	3355	St. Aubyn
		3356	Sir Stafford
3313	Jupiter	3357	Trelawney
3314	Mersey	3358	Tremayne
3315	Quantock	3359	Tregeagle
3316	St. Columb	3360	Torquay
3317	Somerset	3361	Edward VII
3318	Vulcan	3362	Albert Brassey
3319	Weymouth	3363	Baldwin/Alfred Baldwin
3320	Avalon	3364	Bibby/Frank Bibby
3321	Brasenose	3365	C. G. Mott/Charles Grey Mott
3322	Eclipse		
3323	Etona	3366	Earl of Cork
3324	Glastonbury	3367	Evan Llewellyn
3325	Kenilworth	3368	Ernest Palmer/Sir Ernest Palmer
3326	Laira		
3327	Marco Polo	3369	MacIver/David MacIver
3328	Marazion	3370	Sir John Llewelyn
3329	Mars	3371	Sir Massey/Sir Massey Lopes
3330	Orion		
3331	Pegasus	3372	Sir Nigel/Sir N. Kingscote
3332	Pluto		
3333	Perseus	3373	Sir W. H. Wills/Sir William Henry
3334	Tavy		
3335	Tregothnan	3374	Walter Long
3336	Titan	3375	Sir Watkin Wynn
3337	The Wolf	3376	River Plym
3338	Swift	3377	Penzance
3339	Sedgemoor	3378	River Tawe
3340	Camel	3379	River Fal
3341	Blasius	3380	River Yealm
3342	Bonaventura	3381	Birkenhead
3343	Camelot	3382	Cardiff
3344	Dartmouth	3383	Ilfracombe
3345	Exeter/Royal Sovereign/Smeaton	3384	Liverpool/Swindon
		3385	Newport
3346	Godolphin	3386	Paddington
3347	Kingsbridge	3387	Reading
3348	Launceston	3388	Swansea
3349	Lyonesse	3389	Taunton
3350	Newlyn	3390	Wolverhampton
3351	One and All	3391	Dominion of Canada
3352	Pendragon	3392	New Zealand
3353	Plymouth/Pershore Plum	3393	Australia
3354	Restormel	3394	Albany

Later Number	Name	Later Number	Name
3395	Tasmania	3417	Francis Mildmay/Lord Mildmay of Flete
3396	Natal/Natal Colony		
3397	Toronto	3418	Sir Arthur Yorke
3398	Montreal	3422	Aberystwyth
3399	Ottawa	3430	Inchcape
3400	Winnipeg	3434	Joseph Shaw
3401	Vancouver	3439	Weston-super-Mare
3402	Jamaica	3441	Blackbird
3403	Trinidad	3442	Bullfinch
3404	Barbados	3443	Chaffinch
3405	Empire of India	3444	Cormorant
3406	Calcutta	3445	Flamingo
3407	Madras	3446	Goldfinch
3408	Bombay	3447	Jackdaw
3409	Queensland	3448	Kingfisher
3410	Columbia	3449	Nightingale
3411	Stanley Baldwin	3450	Peacock
3412	John G. Griffiths	3451	Pelican
3413	James Mason	3452	Penguin
3414	A. H. Mills/Sir Edward Elgar	3453	Seagull
		3454	Skylark
3415	George A. Wills	3455	Starling
3416	John W. Wilson		

In a number of cases the names were subsequently removed for the same reasons which applied to the 'Duke of Cornwall' class.

Nos. 3321–3360 were provided with the composite name and number plates on the cabsides, the remainder being the standard curved splasher nameplates.

DEAN 7′ 0″ 4-4-0's

A class of four engines whose real history began in 1894, when although nominally rebuilds of experimental 2-4-0 engines (two of which were tandem compounds and three of them built to the broad gauge), they appeared as practically new engines of a handsome 4-4-0 design with outside frames.

Old No.	New No.	Names
7	4171	Armstrong
8	4172	Gooch
14	4170	Charles Saunders
16	4169	Brunel

They were eventually rebuilt with 6′ 8½″ driving wheels and incorporated in the Badminton/Atbara series, the next class to be dealt with. They lasted until 1928–1930.

BADMINTON/ATBARA CLASS 4-4-0's

The various series of these locomotives appeared between 1897 and 1891, more or less concurrently with the 'Bulldog' classes already dealt with, and followed similar lines, the main difference being the provision of straight frames from engines 4120 onwards. In the same way Nos. 4120-4145 had the combined cabside name and number plates, the rest being the standard curved nameplates over the splashers.

Later Number	*Name*	*Later Number*	*Name*
4100	Badminton	—	Old 3382 Mafeking[1]
4101	Barrington	4129	Kekewich
4102	Blenheim	4130	Omdurman
4103	Bessborough	4131	Powerful
4104	Cambria	4132	Pembroke
4105	Earl Cawdor	4133	Roberts
4106	Grosvenor	4134	Sir Redvers
4107	Hubbard/Alexander Hubbard	4135	Sir Daniel/Pretoria
4108	Hotspur	4136	Terrible
4109	Monarch	4137	Wolseley
4110	Mortimer/Charles Mortimer	4138	White/Powerful/White
4111	Marlborough	4139	Auckland
4112	Oxford	4140	Adelaide
4113	Samson	4141	Aden
4114	Shelburne	4142	Brisbane
4115	Shrewsbury	4143	Cape Town
4116	Savernake	4144	Colombo
4117	Shakespeare	4145	Dunedin
4118	Waterford	4146	Sydney
4119	Wynnstay	4147	St. Johns
4120	Atbara/Maine/Royal Sovereign/Atbara	4148	Singapore
4121	Baden Powell/Pretoria/ Britannia/Kitchener	4149	Auricula
		4150	Begonia
4122	Conqueror/Edgcumbe/ Colonel Edgcumbe	4151	Calceolaria
		4152	Calendula
4123	Herschell	4153	Camellia
4124	Kitchener	4154	Campanula
4125	Khartoum	4155	Cineraria
4126	Kimberley	4156	Gardenia
4127	Ladysmith	4157	Lobelia
4128	Maine	4158	Petunia
		4159	Anemone
		4160	Carnation
		4161	Hyacinthe/Hyacinth

[1] This engine was scrapped in 1911 as the result of an accident and never received a number in the 4100 series under the later renumbering scheme. It is shown in the position as it came between Maine (old No. 3381) and Kekewich (old No. 3383).

Later Number	Name	Later Number	Name
4162	Marguerite	3707	Malta
4163	Marigold	3708	Ophir/Killarney
4164	Mignonette	3709	Quebec
4165	Narcissus	3710	City of Bath
4166	Polyanthus	3711	City of Birmingham
4167	Primrose	3712	City of Bristol
4168	Stephanotis	3713	City of Chester
3700	Durban	3714	City of Gloucester
3701	Gibraltar	3715	City of Hereford
3702	Halifax	3716	City of London
3703	Hobart	3717	City of Truro
3704	Lyttleton/Lyttelton	3718	City of Winchester
3705	Mauritius	3719	City of Exeter
3706	Melbourne		

All of these engines, apart from 'Mafeking', were scrapped between 1927 and 1931, excepting of course the famous 'City of Truro', now preserved in Swindon Museum. This engine ran with its original number, 3440, during its restored working period, 1957–61.

CHURCHWARD 4-4-0's 'COUNTY' CLASS

Churchward's design of outside cylinder 4-4-0 with standard 6′ 8½″ wheels for express work. Built 1904–1912 and withdrawn between 1930 and 1933.

Later Number	Name	Later Number	Name
3800	County of Middlesex	3820	County of Worcester
3801	County Carlow	3821	County of Bedford
3802	County Clare	3822	County of Brecon
3803	County Cork	3823	County of Carnarvon
3804	County Dublin	3824	County of Cornwall
3805	County Kerry	3825	County of Denbigh
3806	County Kildare	3826	County of Flint
3807	County Kilkenny	3827	County of Gloucester
3808	County Limerick	3828	County of Hereford
3809	County Wexford	3829	County of Merioneth
3810	County Wicklow	3830	County of Oxford
3811	County of Bucks	3831	County of Berks
3812	County of Cardigan	3832	County of Wilts
3813	County of Carmarthen	3833	County of Dorset
3814	County of Cheshire/ County of Chester	3834	County of Somerset
		3835	County of Devon
3815	County of Hants	3836	County of Warwick
3816	County of Leicester	3837	County of Stafford
3817	County of Monmouth	3838	County of Glamorgan
3818	County of Radnor	3839	County of Pembroke
3819	County of Salop		

COMPOUND ATLANTICS

These engines, imported from France in 1903/5 to the design of the successful 'Nord' Atlantics for testing the merits of compound versus simple engines.

102 La France   103 President   104 Alliance

They did good work on the G.W.R., but eventually Churchward decided in favour of simple as against compound propulsion. They lasted until 1926–1928.

CHURCHWARD 2 CYLINDER 4-6-0's

Dean's No. 100 of 1902 was the first of the long line of G.W.R. express passenger and mixed traffic 4-6-0's, of many classes and of both 2 and 4 cylinder varieties, now summarised in the following pages, all of which without exception bore names.

No. 100 was the prototype of what later became known as the 'Saint' class, which eventually comprised the following engines:

Number	Name	Number	Name
2900	Dean/William Dean	2924	Saint Helena
2901	Lady Superior	2925	Saint Martin
2902	Lady of the Lake	2926	Saint Nicholas
2903	Lady of Lyons	2927	Saint Patrick
2904	Lady Godiva	2928	Saint Sebastian
2905	Lady Macbeth	2929	Saint Stephen
2906	Lady of Lynn	2930	Saint Vincent
2907	Lady Disdain	2931	Arlington Court
2908	Lady of Quality	2932	Ashton Court
2909	Lady of Provence	2933	Bibury Court
2910	Lady of Shalott	2934	Butleigh Court
2911	Saint Agatha	2935	Caynham Court
2912	Saint Ambrose	2936	Cefntilla Court
2913	Saint Andrew	2937	Clevedon Court
2914	Saint Augustine	2938	Corsham Court
2915	Saint Bartholomew	2939	Croome Court
2916	Saint Benedict	2940	Dorney Court
2917	Saint Bernard	2941	Easton Court
2918	Saint Catherine	2942	Fawley Court
2919	Saint Cecilia/Saint Cuthbert	2943	Hampton Court
		2944	Highnam Court
2920	Saint David	2945	Hillingdon Court
2921	Saint Dunstan	2946	Langford Court
2922	Saint Gabriel	2947	Madresfield Court
2923	Saint George	2948	Stackpole Court
		2949	Stanford Court

Number	Name	Number	Name
2950	Taplow Court	2979	Magnet/Quentin Durward
2951	Tawstock Court	2980	Coeur de Lion
2952	Twineham Court	2981	Ivanhoe
2953	Titley Court	2982	Lalla Rookh
2954	Tockenham Court	2983	Red Gauntlet/Redgauntlet
2955	Tortworth Court	2984	Churchill/Viscount Churchill/Guy Mannering
2971	Albion/The Pirate/Albion		
2972	Quicksilver/The Abbot	2985	Winterstoke/Peveril of the Peak
2973	Robins Bolitho		
2974	Barrymore/Lord Barrymore	2986	Robin Hood
		2987	Robertson/Bride of Lammermoor
2975	Viscount Churchill/Sir Ernest Palmer/ Lord Palmer	2988	Rob Roy
		2989	Talisman
2976	Winterstoke	2990	Waverley
2977	Robertson	2998	Vanguard/Ernest Cunard
2978	Kirkland/ Charles J. Hambro		

No. 2900 was the original No. 100 and Nos. 2971–2990 were originally 171–190. No. 2998 (the second engine of the class, built in 1903, following the original 100) was at first No. 98. Nos. 2971, 2972, and 2979–2990 ran for a time as 4-4-2's as a comparison between the merits of the Atlantics and 4-6-0 type for express passenger work.

In 1924 No. 2925 'Saint Martin' was rebuilt with 6′ 0″ wheels and as such became the prototype of the numerous 'Hall' class (see next section) for general mixed traffic work. It received the number 4900 and was in service until 1959. The remainder of the 'Saints' were scrapped between 1931 and 1953.

COLLETT MIXED TRAFFIC 'HALL' CLASS

Following the successful modification of No. 2925 mentioned in the previous section, a big series of engines was turned out between 1928 and 1950 for general mixed traffic duties, all of them named after Halls, mostly after the stately country homes of England, although a few of them, such as 'Queen's Hall' and 'Albert Hall' are obvious exceptions. For war economy reasons Nos. 6916–6970, which were built between 1941 and 1944, were turned out nameless, but they duly received their nameplates later after the end of the war.

Number	Name	Number	Name
4900	Saint Martin	4905	Barton Hall
4901	Adderley Hall	4906	Bradfield Hall
4902	Aldenham Hall	4907	Broughton Hall
4903	Astley Hall	4908	Broome Hall
4904	Binnegar Hall	4909	Blakesley Hall

Number	Name	Number	Name
4910	Blaisdon Hall	4956	Plowden Hall
4911	Bowden Hall	4957	Postlip Hall
4912	Berrington Hall	4958	Priory Hall
4913	Baglan Hall	4959	Purley Hall
4914	Cranmore Hall	4960	Pyle Hall
4915	Condover Hall	4961	Pyrland Hall
4916	Crumlin Hall	4962	Ragley Hall
4917	Crosswood Hall	4963	Rignall Hall
4918	Dartington Hall	4964	Rodwell Hall
4919	Donnington Hall	4965	Rood Ashton Hall
4920	Dumbleton Hall	4966	Shakenhurst Hall
4921	Eaton Hall	4967	Shirenewton Hall
4922	Enville Hall	4968	Shotton Hall
4923	Evenley Hall	4969	Shrugborough Hall
4924	Eydon Hall	4970	Sketty Hall
4925	Eynsham Hall	4971	Stanway Hall
4926	Fairleigh Hall	4972	St. Brides Hall/ Saint Brides Hall
4927	Farnborough Hall		
4928	Gatacre Hall	4973	Sweeney Hall
4929	Goytrey Hall	4974	Talgarth Hall
4930	Hagley Hall	4975	Umberslade Hall
4931	Hanbury Hall	4976	Warfield Hall
4932	Hatherton Hall	4977	Watcombe Hall
4933	Himley Hall	4978	Westwood Hall
4934	Hindlip Hall	4979	Wootton Hall
4935	Ketley Hall	4980	Wrottesley Hall
4936	Kinlet Hall	4981	Abberley Hall
4937	Lanelay Hall	4982	Acton Hall
4938	Liddington Hall	4983	Albert Hall
4939	Littleton Hall	4984	Albrighton Hall
4940	Ludford Hall	4985	Allersley Hall/ Allesley Hall
4941	Llangedwyn Hall		
4942	Maindy Hall	4986	Aston Hall
4943	Marrington Hall	4987	Brockley Hall
4944	Middleton Hall	4988	Bulwell Hall
4945	Milligan Hall	4989	Cherwell Hall
4946	Moseley Hall	4990	Clifton Hall
4947	Nanhoran Hall	4991	Cobham Hall
4948	Northwick Hall	4992	Crosby Hall
4949	Packwood Hall	4993	Dalton Hall
4950	Patshull Hall	4994	Downton Hall
4951	Pendeford Hall	4995	Euston Hall
4952	Peplow Hall	4996	Eden Hall
4953	Pitchford Hall	4997	Elton Hall
4954	Plaish Hall	4998	Eyton Hall
4955	Plaspower Hall	4999	Gopsal Hall

Number	Name	Number	Name
5900	Hinderton Hall	5946	Marwell Hall
5901	Hazel Hall	5947	Saint Benets Hall/
5902	Howick Hall		Saint Benet's Hall
5903	Keele Hall	5948	Siddington Hall
5904	Kelham Hall	5949	Trematon Hall
5905	Knowsley Hall	5950	Wardley Hall
5906	Lawton Hall	5951	Clyffe Hall
5907	Marble Hall	5952	Cogan Hall
5908	Moreton Hall	5953	Dunley Hall
5909	Newton Hall	5954	Faendre Hall
5910	Park Hall	5955	Garth Hall
5911	Preston Hall	5956	Horsley Hall
5912	Queens Hall/Queen's Hall	5957	Hutton Hall
5913	Rushton Hall	5958	Knolton Hall
5914	Ripon Hall	5959	Mawley Hall
5915	Trentham Hall	5960	Saint Edmund Hall
5916	Trinity Hall	5961	Toynbee Hall
5917	Westminster Hall	5962	Wantage Hall
5918	Walton Hall	5963	Wimpole Hall
5919	Worsley Hall	5964	Wolseley Hall
5920	Wycliffe Hall	5965	Woollas Hall
5921	Bingley Hall	5966	Ashford Hall
5922	Caxton Hall	5967	Bickmarsh Hall
5923	Colston Hall	5968	Cory Hall
5924	Dinton Hall	5969	Honington Hall
5925	Eastcote Hall	5970	Hengrave Hall
5926	Grotrian Hall	5971	Merevale Hall
5927	Guild Hall	5972	Olton Hall
5928	Haddon Hall	5973	Rolleston Hall
5929	Hanham Hall	5974	Wallsworth Hall
5930	Hannington Hall	5975	Winslow Hall
5931	Hatherton Hall	5976	Ashwicke Hall
5932	Haydon Hall	5977	Beckford Hall
5933	Kingsway Hall	5978	Bodinnick Hall
5934	Kneller Hall	5979	Cruckton Hall
5935	Norton Hall	5980	Dingley Hall
5936	Oakley Hall	5981	Frensham Hall
5937	Stanford Hall	5982	Harrington Hall
5938	Stanley Hall	5983	Henley Hall
5939	Tangley Hall	5984	Linden Hall
5940	Whitbourne Hall	5985	Mostyn Hall
5941	Campion Hall	5986	Arbury Hall
5942	Doldowlod Hall	5987	Brocket Hall
5943	Elmdon Hall	5988	Bostock Hall
5944	Ickenham Hall	5989	Cransley Hall
5945	Leckhampton Hall	5990	Dorford Hall

Number	Name	Number	Name
5991	Gresham Hall	6937	Conyngham Hall
5992	Horton Hall	6938	Corndean Hall
5993	Kirby Hall	6939	Calveley Hall
5994	Roydon Hall	6940	Didlington Hall
5995	Wick Hall	6941	Fillongley Hall
5996	Mytton Hall	6942	Eshton Hall
5997	Sparkford Hall	6943	Farnley Hall
5998	Trevor Hall	6944	Fledborough Hall
5999	Wollaton Hall	6945	Glasfryn Hall
6900	Abney Hall	6946	Heatherden Hall
6901	Arley Hall	6947	Helmingham Hall
6902	Butlers Hall	6948	Holbrooke Hall
6903	Belmont Hall	6949	Haberfield Hall
6904	Charfield Hall	6950	Kingsthorpe Hall
6905	Claughton Hall	6951	Impney Hall
6906	Chicheley Hall	6952	Kimberley Hall
6907	Davenham Hall	6953	Leighton Hall
6908	Downham Hall	6954	Lotherton Hall
6909	Frewin Hall	6955	Lydcott Hall
6910	Gossington Hall	6956	Mottram Hall
6911	Holker Hall	6957	Norcliffe Hall
6912	Helmster Hall	6958	Oxburgh Hall
6913	Levens Hall	6959	Peatling Hall
6914	Langton Hall	6960	Raveningham Hall
6915	Mursley Hall	6961	Stedham Hall
6916	Misterton Hall	6962	Soughton Hall
6917	Oldlands Hall	6963	Throwley Hall
6918	Sandon Hall	6964	Thornbridge Hall
6919	Tylney Hall	6965	Thirlestaine Hall
6920	Barningham Hall	6966	Witchingham Hall
6921	Borwick Hall	6967	Willesley Hall
6922	Burton Hall	6968	Woodcock Hall
6923	Croxteth Hall	6969	Wraysbury Hall
6924	Grantley Hall	6970	Whaddon Hall
6925	Hackness Hall	6971	Athelhampton Hall
6926	Holkham Hall	6972	Beningbrough Hall
6927	Lilford Hall	6973	Bricklehampton Hall
6928	Underley Hall	6974	Bryngwyn Hall
6929	Whorlton Hall	6975	Capesthorne Hall
6930	Aldersey Hall	6976	Graythwaite Hall
6931	Aldborough Hall	6977	Grundisburgh Hall
6932	Burwarton Hall	6978	Haroldstone Hall
6933	Birtles Hall	6979	Helperly Hall
6934	Beachamwell Hall	6980	Llanrumney Hall
6935	Browsholme Hall	6981	Marbury Hall
6936	Breccles Hall	6982	Melmerby Hall

Number	Name	Number	Name
6983	Otterington Hall	7907	Hart Hall
6984	Owsden Hall	7908	Henshall Hall
6985	Parwick Hall	7909	Heveningham Hall
6986	Rydal Hall	7910	Hown Hall
6987	Shervington Hall	7911	Lady Margaret Hall
6988	Swithland Hall	7912	Little Linford Hall
6989	Wightwick Hall	7913	Little Wyrley Hall
6990	Witherslack Hall	7914	Lleweni Hall
6991	Acton Burnell Hall	7915	Mere Hall
6992	Arborfield Hall	7916	Mobberley Hall
6993	Arthog Hall	7917	North Aston Hall
6994	Baggrave Hall	7918	Rhose Wood Hall
6995	Benthall Hall	7919	Runter Hall
6996	Blackwell Hall	7920	Coney Hall
6997	Bryn-Ivor Hall	7921	Edstone Hall
6998	Burton Agnes Hall	7922	Salford Hall
6999	Capel Dewi Hall	7923	Speke Hall
7900	St. Peter's Hall	7924	Thornycroft Hall
7901	Dodington Hall	7925	Westol Hall
7902	Eaton Mascot Hall	7926	Willey Hall
7903	Foremarke Hall	7927	Willington Hall
7904	Fountains Hall	7928	Wolf Hall
7905	Fowey Hall	7929	Wyke Hall
7906	Fron Hall		

The original conversion, No. 4900, was scrapped in 1959, and one or two others followed shortly afterward but scrapping on a large scale did not commence until 1962.

'GRANGE' CLASS MIXED TRAFFIC 4-6-0's

A new class of light mixed traffic 4-6-0 built between 1936 and 1939 to replace the existing 2-6-0 engines. It was intended that there should be many more of the class but construction was suspended on the outbreak of war and never resumed.

Number	Name	Number	Name
6800	Arlington Grange	6810	Blakemere Grange
6801	Aylburton Grange	6811	Cranbourne Grange
6802	Bampton Grange	6812	Chesford Grange
6803	Bucklebury Grange	6813	Eastbury Grange
6804	Brockington Grange	6814	Enbourne Grange
6805	Broughton Grange	6815	Frilford Grange
6806	Blackwell Grange	6816	Frankton Grange
6807	Birchwood Grange	6817	Gwenddwr Grange
6808	Beenham Grange	6818	Hardwick Grange
6809	Burghclere Grange	6819	Highnam Grange

Number	Name	Number	Name
6820	Kingstone Grange	6850	Cleeve Grange
6821	Leaton Grange	6851	Hurst Grange
6822	Manton Grange	6852	Headbourne Grange
6823	Oakley Grange	6853	Morehampton Grange
6824	Ashley Grange	6854	Roundhill Grange
6825	Llanvair Grange	6855	Saighton Grange
6826	Nannerth Grange	6856	Stowe Grange
6827	Llanfrechfa Grange	6857	Tudor Grange
6828	Trellech Grange	6858	Woolston Grange
6829	Burmingham Grange	6859	Yiewsley Grange
6830	Buckenhill Grange	6860	Aberporth Grange
6831	Bearley Grange	6861	Crynant Grange
6832	Brockton Grange	6862	Derwent Grange
6833	Calcot Grange	6863	Dolhywel Grange
6834	Dummer Grange	6864	Dymock Grange
6835	Eastham Grange	6865	Hopton Grange
6836	Estevarney Grange	6866	Morfa Grange
6837	Forthampton Grange	6867	Peterston Grange
6838	Goodmoor Grange	6868	Penrhos Grange
6839	Hewell Grange	6869	Resolven Grange
6840	Hazeley Grange	6870	Bodicote Grange
6841	Marlas Grange	6871	Bourton Grange
6842	Nunhold Grange	6872	Crawley Grange
6843	Poulton Grange	6873	Caradoc Grange
6844	Penhydd Grange	6874	Haughton Grange
6845	Paviland Grange	6875	Hindford Grange
6846	Ruckley Grange	6876	Kingsland Grange
6847	Tidmarsh Grange	6877	Llanfair Grange
6848	Toddington Grange	6878	Longford Grange
6849	Walton Grange	6879	Overton Grange

Withdrawal commenced in 1960.

'MANOR' CLASS 4-6-0's

Similar to the 'Grange' class just described, but lighter in construction and with a greater route availability.

Like the 'Granges', it was intended that many more should be constructed to replace the mixed traffic 2-6-0 engines, but in this case although only 20 had appeared before the outbreak of war, a further ten were in fact built in 1950, after Nationalisation. The fact that the programme was never completed is however well illustrated by the fact that the great majority of the allocated names are in the first half of the alphabet, it being immediately noticeable that, as in the case of the 'Granges' (and going back to an earlier period, with the 'Saints' and 'Stars', and again more recently with the 'Halls' and,

'Castles') it had become the practice to allocate the names of the various batches of engines turned out under the general 'Key' name classes in alphabetical order.

Number	Name	Number	Name
7800	Torquay Manor	7815	Fritwell Manor
7801	Anthony Manor	7816	Frilsham Manor
7802	Bradley Manor	7817	Garsington Manor
7803	Barcote Manor	7818	Granville Manor
7804	Baydon Manor	7819	Hinton Manor
7805	Broome Manor	7820	Dinmore Manor
7806	Cockington Manor	7821	Ditcheat Manor
7807	Compton Manor	7822	Foxcote Manor
7808	Cookham Manor	7823	Hook Norton Manor
7809	Childrey Manor	7824	Iford Manor
7810	Draycott Manor	7825	Lechlade Manor
7811	Dunley Manor	7826	Longworth Manor
7812	Erlestoke Manor	7827	Lydham Manor
7813	Freshford Manor	7828	Odney Manor
7814	Fringford Manor	7829	Ramsbury Manor

Nos. 7800–7819 were turned out in 1938–9 and 7820–7829 in 1950.

HAWKSWORTH 6′ 3″ 4-6-0's

A series of 2 cylinder 4-6-0's built by Hawksworth in 1945–1947, intended for express passenger work. Although generally following Great Western traditions, they were unusual in being provided with one long continuous splasher which necessitated the use of a rectangular nameplate.

Number	Name	Number	Name
1000	County of Middlesex	1015	County of Gloucester
1001	County of Bucks	1016	County of Hants
1002	County of Berks	1017	County of Hereford
1003	County of Wilts	1018	County of Leicester
1004	County of Somerset	1019	County of Merioneth
1005	County of Devon	1020	County of Monmouth
1006	County of Cornwall	1021	County of Montgomery
1007	County of Brecknock	1022	County of Northampton
1008	County of Cardigan	1023	County of Oxford
1009	County of Carmarthen	1024	County of Pembroke
1010	County of Carnarvon/	1025	County of Radnor
	County of Caernarvon	1026	County of Salop
1011	County of Chester	1027	County of Stafford
1012	County of Denbigh	1028	County of Warwick
1013	County of Dorset	1029	County of Worcester
1014	County of Glamorgan		

CHURCHWARD 4 CYLINDER 4-6-0's 'STAR' CLASS

The original engine, No. 40, was turned out in 1906 as a 4-4-2, in order to provide direct comparison with the three French Atlantics already described. After running in this form for three years it was converted to 4-6-0 in conformity with several batches of new engines which had already appeared, constructed to this wheel arrangement. No. 40 later became 4000 and the whole class comprised seventy three engines, as follows:—

Number	Name	Number	Name
4000	North Star	4024	King James/Dutch Monarch
4001	Dog Star	4025	King Charles/Italian Monarch
4002	Evening Star	4026	King Richard/Japanese Monarch
4003	Lode Star		
4004	Morning Star	4027	King Henry/Norwegian Monarch
4005	Polar Star		
4006	Red Star	4028	King John/Roumanian Monarch
4007	Rising Star/Swallowfield Park		
		4029	King Stephen/Spanish Monarch
4008	Royal Star		
4009	Shooting Star/Lloyds	4030	King Harold/Swedish Monarch
4010	Western Star		
4011	Knight of the Garter	4031	Queen Mary
4012	Knight of the Thistle	4032	Queen Alexandra
4013	Knight of St. Patrick	4033	Queen Victoria
4014	Knight of the Bath	4034	Queen Adelaide
4015	Knight of St. John	4035	Queen Charlotte
4016	Knight of the Golden Fleece/The Somerset Light Infantry (Prince Albert's)	4036	Queen Elizabeth
		4037	Queen Philippa/The South Wales Borderers
4017	Knight of the Black Eagle/Knight of Liege*	4038	Queen Berengaria
		4039	Queen Matilda
4018	Knight of the Grand Cross	4040	Queen Boadicea
4019	Knight Templar	4041	Prince of Wales
4020	Knight Commander	4042	Prince Albert
4021	King Edward/British Monarch	4043	Prince Henry
		4044	Prince George
4022	King William/Belgian Monarch	4045	Prince John
		4046	Princess Mary
4023	King George/Danish Monarch		

* The name of No. 4017 was altered early in the first world war as 'The Knight of the Black Eagle' was of German origin. 'Knight of Liege' was chosen as a tribute to the heroism of the Belgians.

Number	Name	Number	Name
4047	Princess Louise	4061	Glastonbury Abbey
4048	Princess Victoria/Princess Mary/Princess Victoria	4062	Malmesbury Abbey
		4063	Bath Abbey
4049	Princess Maud	4064	Reading Abbey
4050	Princess Alice	4065	Evesham Abbey
4051	Princess Helena	4066	Malvern Abbey/Sir Robert Horne/Viscount Horne
4052	Princess Beatrice		
4053	Princess Alexandra		
4054	Princess Charlotte	4067	Tintern Abbey
4055	Princess Sophia	4068	Llanthony Abbey
4056	Princess Margaret	4069	Margam Abbey/ Westminster Abbey
4057	Princess Elizabeth		
4058	Princess Augusta	4070	Neath Abbey
4059	Princess Patricia	4071	Cleeve Abbey
4060	Princess Eugenie	4072	Tresco Abbey

No. 4009 was later renumbered 100A1, when its name was changed to 'Lloyds'. The King batch, Nos. 4021–4030 were renamed 'Monarchs' in 1927 after the appearance of the well known 'King George V' class. The names of 4022/3/5/6 were removed during the second world war for obvious reasons, and the engines thereafter remained nameless. Nos. 4000, 4009, 4016, 4032 and 4037 were eventually rebuilt as 'Castle' class, retaining the same numbers, and the last ten of the batch of twelve 'Abbeys'. Nos. 4063–4072 were similarly treated *en bloc* but in this case renumbered 5083–5092. Nos. 4061 and 4062 remained 'Star' class engines until withdrawal.

Scrapping began in 1934, and the last unrebuilt engine, No. 4003, was retained on withdrawal in 1951 and it is now preserved in Swindon Museum.

Some of the 'Castle' rebuilds lasted somewhat longer, in fact No. 4037 was not withdrawn until 1962, at which time several of the 'Abbeys' were still in service.

COLLETT 4 CYLINDER 4-6-0's 'CASTLE' CLASS

These were a natural development of the 'Stars', and may be said to rank among the most famous of classes ever to run.

The first engine appeared from Swindon in 1923, and the class was multiplied steadily right up to 1950, three years after Nationalisation.

Number	Name	Number	Name
4073	Caerphilly Castle	4081	Warwick Castle
4074	Caldicot Castle	4082	Windsor Castle
4075	Cardiff Castle	4083	Abbotsbury Castle
4076	Carmarthen Castle	4084	Aberystwyth Castle
4077	Chepstow Castle	4085	Berkeley Castle
4078	Pembroke Castle	4086	Builth Castle
4079	Pendennis Castle	4087	Cardigan Castle
4080	Powderham Castle	4088	Dartmouth Castle

Number	Name	Number	Name
4089	Donnington Castle	5033	Broughton Castle
4090	Dorchester Castle	5034	Corfe Castle
4091	Dudley Castle	5035	Coity Castle
4092	Dunraven Castle	5036	Lyonshall Castle
4093	Dunster Castle	5037	Monmouth Castle
4094	Dynevor Castle	5038	Morlais Castle
4095	Harlech Castle	5039	Rhuddlan Castle
4096	Highclere Castle	5040	Stokesay Castle
4097	Kenilworth Castle	5041	Tiverton Castle
4098	Kidwelly Castle	5042	Winchester Castle
4099	Kilgerran Castle	5043	Barbury Castle/Earl of Mount Edgcumbe
5000	Launceston Castle		
5001	Llandovery Castle	5044	Beverston Castle/Earl of Dunraven
5002	Ludlow Castle		
5003	Lulworth Castle	5045	Bridgwater Castle/Earl of Dudley
5004	Llanstephan Castle		
5005	Manorbier Castle	5046	Clifford Castle/Earl Cawdor
5006	Tregenna Castle	5047	Compton Castle/Earl of Dartmouth
5007	Rougemont Castle		
5008	Raglan Castle	5048	Cranbrook Castle/Earl of Devon
5009	Shrewsbury Castle		
5010	Restormel Castle	5049	Denbigh Castle/Earl of Plymouth
5011	Tintagel Castle		
5012	Berry Pomeroy Castle	5050	Devizes Castle/Earl of St. Germans
5013	Abergavenny Castle		
5014	Goodrich Castle	5051	Drysllwyn Castle/Earl Bathurst
5015	Kingswear Castle		
5016	Montgomery Castle	5052	Eastnor Castle/Earl of Radnor
5017	St. Donats Castle/The Gloucestershire Regiment 28th/61st		
		5053	Bishop's Castle/Earl Cairns
5018	St. Mawes Castle	5054	Lamphey Castle/Earl of Ducie
5019	Treago Castle		
5020	Trematon Castle	5055	Lydford Castle/Earl of Eldon
5021	Whittington Castle		
5022	Wigmore Castle	5056	Ogmore Castle/Earl of Powis
5023	Brecon Castle		
5024	Carew Castle	5057	Penrice Castle/Earl Waldegrave
5025	Chirk Castle		
5026	Criccieth Castle	5058	Newport Castle/Earl of Clancarty
5027	Farleigh Castle		
5028	Llantilio Castle	5059	Powis Castle/Earl St. Aldwyn
5029	Nunney Castle		
5030	Shirburn Castle	5060	Sarum Castle/Earl of Berkeley
5031	Totnes Castle		
5032	Usk Castle	5061	Sudeley Castle/Earl of Birkenhead

Number	Name
5062	Tenby Castle/Earl of Shaftesbury
5063	Thornbury Castle/Earl Baldwin
5064	Tretower Castle/Bishops Castle
5065	Upton Castle/Newport Castle
5066	Wardour Castle/Sir Felix Pole
5067	St. Fagans Castle
5068	Beverston Castle
5069	Isambard Kingdom Brunel
5070	Sir Daniel Gooch
5071	Clifford Castle/Spitfire
5072	Compton Castle/ Hurricane
5073	Cranbrook Castle/ Blenheim
5074	Denbigh Castle/Hampden
5075	Devizes Castle/ Wellington
5076	Drysllwyn Castle/ Gladiator
5077	Eastnor Castle/Fairey Battle
5078	Lamphey Castle/ Beaufort
5079	Lydford Castle/Lysander
5080	Ogmore Castle/Defiant
5081	Penrice Castle/Lockheed Hudson
5082	Powis Castle/Swordfish
5083	Bath Abbey
5084	Reading Abbey
5085	Evesham Abbey
5086	Viscount Horne
5087	Tintern Abbey
5088	Llanthony Abbey
5089	Westminster Abbey
5090	Neath Abbey
5091	Cleeve Abbey
5092	Tresco Abbey
5093	Upton Castle
5094	Tretower Castle

Number	Name
5095	Barbury Castle
5096	Bridgwater Castle
5097	Sarum Castle
5098	Clifford Castle
5099	Compton Castle
7000	Viscount Portal
7001	Denbigh Castle/Sir James Milne
7002	Devizes Castle
7003	Elmley Castle
7004	Eastnor Castle
7005	Lamphey Castle/Sir Edward Elgar
7006	Lydford Castle
7007	Ogmore Castle/Great Western
7008	Swansea Castle
7009	Athelney Castle
7010	Avondale Castle
7011	Banbury Castle
7012	Barry Castle
7013	Bristol Castle
7014	Caerhayes Castle
7015	Carn Brea Castle
7016	Chester Castle
7017	G. J. Churchward
7018	Drysllwyn Castle
7019	Fowey Castle
7020	Gloucester Castle
7021	Haverfordwest Castle
7022	Hereford Castle
7023	Penrice Castle
7024	Powis Castle
7025	Sudeley Castle
7026	Tenby Castle
7027	Thornbury Castle
7028	Cadbury Castle
7029	Clun Castle
7030	Cranbrook Castle
7031	Cromwell's Castle
7032	Denbigh Castle
7033	Hartlebury Castle
7034	Ince Castle
7035	Ogmore Castle
7036	Taunton Castle
7037	Swindon

The L.N.W.R. War Memorial engine 'Patriot'.

L.N.W.R. 'Coronation', the 5000th engine built at Crewe works, and bearing a numberplate to correspond, although its official number in the stock list was 1800.

An unusual type of nameplate for a L.N.W.R. engine.

L.N.W.R. narrow gauge works engine at Crewe works.

L. & Y.R. narrow gauge works engine at Horwic

L.N.W.R. standard type of nameplate typified by 'Precursor' class engine 366.

Leek and Manifold Valley Light Railway—combir name, number and works plate.

[L.P.C.

One of the three narrow gauge North Stafford Railway engines employed in Caldon Low Quarries. The other two were 'Frog' and 'Bobs'.

[W. H. Whitw

L.N.W.R. narrow gauge works engines 'Jim Crc and 'Platelayer'.

Midland Railway Johnson single 'Princess of Wales'.

[*L.P.C.*

Midland Railway Johnson 4-4-0 'Beatrice'.

[*L.P.C.*

[*L.P.C.*

L.T. & S.R. 4-4-2T No. 54. In common with other Tilbury engines it lost its name on becoming M.R. No. 2161

Caledonian Railway—the first 'Dunalastair'.

Caledonian Railway—McIntosh 4-6-0 'Sir James Thompson'.

Glasgow and South Western Railway 'Lord Glenarthur'.

It is seen that a considerable amount of renaming has occurred, and it will be noticed that the name 'Ogmore Castle' has actually appeared on four different engines of the class, Nos. 5056, 5080, 7007 and finally 7035.

In 1952, No. 7013, Bristol Castle exchanged name and number plates with No. 4082 Windsor Castle for the purpose of working King George VI's funeral train, and the change became permanent.

Scrapping of the class began in 1959, and by 1962 heavy inroads were being made upon them. Nos. 4079 and 7029 have been preserved privately, and No. 4073 is in the Science Museum.

CHURCHWARD 4-6-2

The Great Western's only 'Pacific' class locomotive, No. 111 The Great Bear, was built at Swindon in 1908. Owing to weight restrictions it had a very low route availability and it was reconstructed in 1924 as a standard 4-6-0 'Castle'. It continued to carry the same number but was renamed 'Viscount Churchill'. It was scrapped in 1953.

COLLETT 'KING' CLASS 4-6-0's

Although the design appeared as long ago as 1927, this class was destined to be the largest and most powerful of the long line of Great Western 4-6-0's.

Thirty engines were turned out between 1927 and 1930, named after the reigning Kings of England in reverse historical order. This accounts for the renaming of the last two engines when King Edward VIII and King George VI respectively ascended the throne.

Number	Name	Number	Name
6000	King George V	6016	King Edward V
6001	King Edward VII	6017	King Edward IV
6002	King William IV	6018	King Henry VI
6003	King George IV	6019	King Henry V
6004	King George III	6020	King Henry IV
6005	King George II	6021	King Richard II
6006	King George I	6022	King Edward III
6007	King William III	6023	King Edward II
6008	King James II	6024	King Edward I
6009	King Charles II	6025	King Henry III
6010	King Charles I	6026	King John
6011	King James I	6027	King Richard I
6012	King Edward VI	6028	King Henry II/King George VI
6013	King Henry VIII		
6014	King Henry VII	6029	King Stephen/King Edward VIII
6015	King Richard III		

No. 6000 visited the U.S.A. in 1927 and received a commemoration bell on the front end, which it still carries.

The class did yeoman service until finally supplanted by diesels, but all were taken out of service during 1962. No. 6000 is preserved.

Very few Great Western engines other than the passenger tender engines just described have borne names since 1900, although many did in earlier years, particularly in broad gauge days.

The exceptions may be summarised as follows:—

1473 Fair Rosamund, one of a numerous class of 0-4-2T's which was built in 1883, and ran till 1935. It acquired its name when working a Royal Special over the Woodstock branch, and retained it thereafter.

1813 Holmwood, a standard 0-6-0T built in 1882 and transferred in 1883 to the Pembroke and Tenby Railway, becoming their No. 7 and acquiring its name. It returned to the G.W.R. in 1896, reassuming its old number, and retained its name through rebuilding successively with saddle and pannier tanks, until withdrawal in 1928.

Three 0-6-4PT's fitted with cranes for yard duties at Swindon and Wolverhampton works. The first two were built in 1901 and the third in 1921. All were withdrawn in 1936.

16   Hercules   17   Cyclops   18   Steropes

The remaining engines, which were all of non G.W.R. origin, were acquired from various small railways taken over by that Company at different periods. These were all prior to the 1923 grouping, and it is somewhat remarkable that of the thousand or so engines then absorbed by the G.W.R. from fifteen different railways, only a small handful from the Burry Port and Gwendraeth Valley, Alexandra Docks, Llanelly Cleobury Mortimer, and Cambrian Railways had names.

GWR No.	Name	Type	Former owning Company	Date of withdrawal
1304	Plynlimmon	2-4-2T	Manchester and Milford	1916
1305	Lady Elizabeth	2-4-0	,,	1906
1306	Cader Idris	2-4-2T	,,	1919
1308	Lady Margaret	2-4-0T	Liskeard and Looe	1948
1311	Cheesewring	0-6-0ST	,,	1919
1312	Kilmar	,,	,,	1914
1317	Emperor	0-6-0ST	South Devon	1905

Nos. 1317-1333 were conversions from broad gauge.

GWR No.	Name	Type	Former owning Company	Date of withdrawal
1318	Python	0-6-0ST	South Devon	1905
1319	Vulcan	,,	,, ,,	1903
1320	Buffalo	,,	,, ,,	1905
1321	Elephant	,,	,, ,,	1904

GWR No.	Name	Type	Former owning Company		Date of withdrawal
1322	Camel	0-6-0ST	South Devon		1903
1323	Dragon	,,	,,	,,	1904
1324	Achilles	,,	,,	,,	1905
1325	Dromedary	,,	,,	,,	1904
1326	Taurus	,,	,,	,,	1905
1327	Owl	0-4-0ST	,,	,,	1913
1328	Goat	,,	,,	,,	1910
1329	Raven	,,	,,	,,	Sold 1910*
1330	Rook	,,	,,	,,	1906
1331	Crow	,,	,,	,,	1907
1332	Lark	,,	,,	,,	1906
1333	Jay	,,	,,	,,	1909
1337	Hook Norton	0-6-0ST	Hook Norton Ironstone Co		1926
1339	Aberystwyth	0-6-0	Manchester and Milford		1906
1353	Gaveller	0-6-0T	Severn & Wye		1903
1354	Severn Bridge	,,	,,	,,	1906
1355	Alan-a-Dale	,,	,,	,,	1905
1356	Will Scarlet	,,	,,	,,	Sold 1912
1357	Maid Marian	,,	,,	,,	1910
1359	Wye	0-4-0T	,,	,,	1910
1361	Pembroke	2-4-0	Pembroke & Tenby		1902
1364	Tenby	0-6-0	,,	,,	1903
1378	Margaret	0-6-0ST	North Pembroke & Fishguard		Sold 1910
1379	Precelly	,,	North Pembroke & Fishguard		Sold 1907
1380	Ringing Rock	,,	North Pembroke & Fishguard		Sold 1912
1385	John Owen	,,	Whitland & Cardigan		Sold 1912
1388	Goonbarrow	,,	Cornwall Mineral		Sold 1911

* No. 1329 went to the Wantage Tramway (see page 172).
† Sold to Gwendreath Valley Railway (not to be confused with the Burry Port and Gwendraeth Valley) becoming their No. 2. Resold to Kidwelly Tinplate Co. in 1923, and although it has not been used for many years it was recently still in existence.

Burry Port and Gwendraeth Valley Railway

(absorbed by G.W.R. at the grouping in 1923)

B.P. & G.V.R. No.	G.W.R. No.	Name	Type	Date of withdrawal
1	2192	Ashburnam	0-6-0ST	1951
3	2193	Burry Port	,,	1952

B.P. & G.V.R. No.	G.W.R. No.	Name	Type	Date of withdrawal
4	2194	Kidwelly	0-6-0ST	1953
5	2195	Cwm Mawr	,,	1953
6	2196	Gwendraeth	,,	1956
7	2176	Pembrey	,,	1955
8	2197	Pioneer	0-6-0T	1952

Llanelly and Mynydd Mawr Railway

Name on L.M.M.	G.W.R. No.	Type	Date of withdrawal
George Waddell	312	0-6-0T	Sold 1935
Tarndune	339	,,	Scrapped 1943
Hilda	359	0-6-0ST	,, 1954
Victory	704	0-6-0T	,, 1944
Ravelston	803	,,	,, 1951
Markland	937	,,	,, 1923
Great Mountain	944	,,	Sold 1929
Seymour Clarke	969	,,	Scrapped 1925
John Waddell	—	,,	Sold 1923
Jeanie Waddell	—	,,	,, 1923

All except 'Hilda' latterly lost their names on the G.W.R. Some of the engines sold out of service were still at work at various collieries as recently as 1960.

Alexandra Docks (Newport and South Wales) Railway

Two small 0-4-0ST's on this line carried names. They were unnumbered on the A.D.R., but came into the G.W.R. stock at the grouping.

G.W.R. No.	Name
1340	Trojan
1341	Alexandra

'Alexandra' had lost its name by 1927, and was scrapped in 1946. No. 1340 'Trojan' however was sold in 1934 and eventually came into the hands of Alders Paper Mills, Tamworth, where it was recently at work still carrying its nameplates and G.W.R. number plates.

Brecon and Merthyr Railway

This line named all of its engines in early days, but discontinued the practice from 1881 onwards, and very few of the originals lasted over the turn of the century. Mention might be made, however, of a 0-6-0ST No. 24 'Cyfarthfa', eventually sold to the Cyfarthfa Ironworks, Merthyr Tydfil, where it continued to work for a number of years. This latter concern named all of its engines 'Cyfarthfa 3', 'Cyfarthfa 4', etc. The works have now long been dismantled.

Cambrian Railways

The few main line engines of the Cambrian which had at one time borne names seem all to have lost them by 1900, and thereafter all of its principal locomotives ran nameless.

In the case, however, of the two narrow gauge lines which it accquired, the names on the Vale of Rheidol were retained for a time, although they had disappeared by the time the Great Western absorbed the line at the grouping. In the case of the Welshpool and Llanfair, the engines still retained their names when taken over by the G.W.R.

The original Vale of Rheidol engines were as follows:

1	Edward VII	2-6-2T	built 1902
2	Prince of Wales	,,	,, ,,
3	Rheidol	2-4-0T	,, 1896

No. 3 was withdrawn in 1923 when taken over by the G.W.R., the other two becoming Nos. 1212 and 1213 in Great Western stock. No. 1212 was scrapped in 1934.

Two further engines of the same design were built at Swindon shortly after the grouping, these were numbered 7 and 8 in G.W.R. list, but for many years were unnamed. In 1956 however the surviving engine of the original stock, No. 1213, was renumbered 9 and its original name restored, the other two at the same time receiving names:—

7 Owain Glyndŵr   8 Llywelyn   9 Prince of Wales

The line is still open in 1967, this 1' 11½" gauge railway being the only narrow gauge section remaining on the nationalised British railway system, with all three engines in service.

The 2' 6" gauge Welshpool and Llanfair Railway possessed two 0-6-0T's:—

W. & L. No.	*G.W.R. No.*	*Name*
1	822	The Earl
2	823	Countess

The names were removed from both engines about 1950. Passenger traffic ceased in 1931, but the line remained open for freight until 1956, when it was closed entirely by B. R. The engines were retained in store however pending efforts by an independent organisation to reopen the line under private auspices, and this project came to fruition in 1962, when the engines were repaired and put back into service. (See page 173).

Mention should be made of three other engines which came into Cambrian ownership in 1904. These were some 0-6-0T's purchased from the small Lambourn Valley Railway, which was acquired by the G.W.R. in 1905, and thereafter became merely one of the numerous branches of that system, running from Newbury to Lambourn.

The engines in question were as follows:—

Cambrian No.	*Name*	*Cambrian No.*	*Name*	*Cambrian No.*	*Name*
26	Ealhswith	35	Aelfred	24	Eadweade

All lost their names when taken over by the Cambrian. They eventually became G.W.R. Nos. 820, 821 and 819 respectively, and the latter engine survived until 1946, when it was broken up at Swindon.

Finally, there was the Mawddwy Railway, which was taken over by the Cambrian in 1911. It possessed two ancient 0-6-0ST's, which had been built in 1865 and 1869, and named respectively

Mawddwy

Disraeli

The second engine was scrapped straight away, but 'Mawddwy' became Cambrian No. 30 (losing its name in the process) and eventually G.W.R. No. 824. It survived until 1940.

Cleobury Mortimer and Ditton Priors Light Railway

	Fleetwood	0-6-0ST	built	1888
1	Burwarton	„	„	1908
2	Cleobury	„	„	1908

Nos. 1 and 2 became G.W.R. 29 and 28 at the grouping, but had lost their names. They lasted until 1953/4.

Corris Railway

This 2′ 3″ gauge line remained independent until 1930, when it was taken over by the G.W.R.

Of its four engines, only one was named, a 0-4-2ST, built by Kerr Stuart in 1921, and known as 'Tattoo', although the name was probably only carried for a short time.

It is now running on the Tal-y-Llyn Railway, having been purchased in 1951 from B.R. when the Corris was closed, and it is now 'Edward Thomas' on that line. It is interesting to observe, incidentally, that it possesses the somewhat unique record of having borne the same number, 4, under four different ownerships, viz. Corris Railway, Great Western, British Railways, and Tal-y-Llyn Railway.

BRITISH RAILWAYS NO. 1

This little known locomotive can best be dealt with here at the conclusion of the Great Western section, as although it was never actually a G.W.R. engine it was allocated to a number in the Western Region series when acquired by British Railways in 1948. It was a small 0-4-0ST purchased from the Ystalyfera tin works, built by Peckett's in 1900, and named 'Hercules'.

As B.R. No. 1 it shunted in Swansea docks until withdrawal in 1954.

II

The London
Midland and Scottish Group

London and North Western Railway

Like its chief rival, the G.W., the L.N.W.R. adopted a consistent policy of naming all its express passenger engines until the last few years of its existence, although in the case of the L.N.W.R. it dated from a much earlier period. In the last years the practice showed signs of dying out, as a large number of 'Prince of Wales' and 'Claughton' class 4-6-0's turned out during the first world war and subsequently never received names, and it may well be that had there been no Grouping the North Western might have eventually abandoned the practice.

The type of nameplate which was introduced about 1850 during Mr McConnell's regime in the first days of the L.N.W.R. remained standard throughout the whole of the Company's existence, with one or two very minor exceptions. This consisted of a brass plate—semi circular or oblong according to the shape of the driving wheel splasher, the invariable position in which it was located, with sunken black lettering.

The actual names chosen for L.N.W. engines did not usually conform to such a consistent pattern as that generally adopted on the G.W., in fact in many cases they seem to have been taken very much at random, comprising all manner of subjects, from the more common personality and place names to Greek Mythology, often interspersed amongst engines of the same class. Many of the names seem to have become established favourites, and re-appeared sometimes with the same number on engines of a new class when the old one bearing the name had been scrapped. The numbering system on the L.N.W., too, was quite different from the G.W. (except in a very few instances, such as the 4-4-0 Compounds, see page 50) in that instead of being in batches a new engine took the first available number left blank by any other engine that happened to have been withdrawn or renumbered into the duplicate list.

At the turn of the century the principal express classes in use were the somewhat erratic Webb compounds of 2-2-2-0 and 2-2-2-2 types, more than supported by the much more reliable 2-4-0 simple engines of the 'Precedent' and other classes. There were also 60 2-2-2 engines of an old design which at that time continued to do much useful work on secondary trains and piloting on the main line. The 4-4-0 Compounds of the 'Jubilee' and 'Alfred the Great' classes had only just begun to appear. Dealing first with the 2-2-2's

40

known as 'Lady of the Lakes' or more popular 'Problems', which dated from 1859–1865, these were as follows:—

Number	Name	Number	Name
1	Saracen	610	Princess Royal
7	Scorpion	612	Princess Alice
28	Prometheus	618	Princess Alexandra
33	Erebus	622	Prince Alfred
44	Harlequin	665	Lord of the Isles
60	Tantalus	667	Marmion
61	Phosphorus	675	Ivanhoe
77	Mersey	719	Outram
97	Atalanta	723	Clive
111	Russell	754	Ethelred
117	Tiger	762	Locke
127	Peel	802	Red Gauntlet
134	Owl	803	Tornado
139	Cygnet	804	Soult
165	Star	806	Waverley
184	Problem	818	Havelock
196	Leander	827	Victoria
218	Wellington	833	Clyde
222	Lily	834	Elgin
229	Watt	837	Faerie Queene
230	Monarch	1427	Edith
234	Mazeppa	1428	Eleanor
279	Stephenson	1429	Alfred Paget
291	Prince of Wales	1430	Pandora
531	Lady of the Lake	1431	Psyche
561	Prince Oscar	1432	Panopea
562	Palmerston	1433	Daphne
563	Combermere	1434	Eunomia
564	Majestic	1435	Fortuna
565	Napoleon	1436	Egeria

This class became extinct in 1907 with the disappearance of No. 618 'Princess Alexandra'.

'CORNWALL'

This engine was constructed at Crewe in 1847 by Francis Trevithick. It is believed to have been originally of the 2-2-2 type, but if so, it was soon altered to a 4-2-2. The boiler was at first underneath the driving axle, only the large wheel diameter of 8' 6" made this possible. It was rebuilt by Ramsbottom in 1858 and remained in ordinary service until 1902, when it was put on to departmental duties hauling an inspectors' saloon.

Originally No. 173, it later became No. 3020, and since its retirement in 1927 has been preserved at Crewe.

The first Webb compounds were a series of 2-2-2-0 engines built between 1882 and 1884:—

Number	Name	Number	Name
66	Experiment	363	Aurania
300	Compound	365	America
301	Economist	366	City of Chicago
302	Velocipede	372	Empress
303	Hydra	374	Emperor
305	Trentham	519	Shooting Star
306	Knowsley	520	Express
307	Victor	1102	Cyclops
310	Sarmatian	1104	Sunbeam
311	Richard Francis Roberts	1111	Messenger
315	Alaska	1113	Hecate
321	Servia	1115	Snake
323	Britannic	1116	Friar
333	Germanic	1117	Penguin
353	Oregon	1120	Apollo

These were followed in 1884–1888 by the 'Dreadnoughts':—

Number	Name	Number	Name
2	City of Carlisle	644	Vesuvius
173	City of Manchester	645	Alchymist
410	City of Liverpool	647	Ambassador
437	City of Chester	648	Swiftsure
503	Dreadnought	659	Rowland Hill
504	Thunderer	885	Himalaya
507	Marchioness of Stafford	1353	City of Edinburgh
508	Titan	1370	City of Glasgow
509	Ajax	1379	Stork
510	Leviathan	1395	Archimedes
511	Achilles	2055	Dunrobin
513	Mammoth	2056	Argus
515	Niagara	2057	Euphrates
545	Tamerlane	2058	Medusa
637	City of New York	2059	Greyhound
638	City of Paris	2060	Vandal
639	City of London	2061	Harpy
640	City of Dublin	2062	Herald
641	City of Lichfield	2063	Huskisson
643	Raven	2064	Autocrat

The final series of 2-2-2-0's came out in 1889 and 1890, and were as follows:—

Number	Name	Number	Name
1301	Teutonic	1306	Ionic
1302	Oceanic	1307	Coptic
1303	Pacific	1309	Adriatic
1304	Jeanie Deans	1311	Celtic
1305	Doric	1312	Gaelic

These were followed by the larger 'Greater Britain' 2-2-2-2's in 1891–1894:—

Number	Name	Number	Name
525	Princess May	772	Richard Trevithick
526	Scottish Chief	2051	George Findlay
527	Henry Bessemer	2052	Prince George
528	Richard Moon	2053	Greater Britain
767	William Cawkwell	2054	Queen Empress

Finally came the 'John Hick' class 2-2-2-2's, similar to the 'Greater Britain', but with 6' 3" driving wheels instead of 7' 1":—

Number	Name	Number	Name
20	John Hick	1536	Hugh Myddleton
1505	Richard Arkwright	1548	John Penn
1512	Henry Cort	1549	John Rennie
1534	William Froude	1557	Thomas Savery
1535	Henry Maudslay	1559	William Siemens

Generally speaking, all of these non-coupled 3-cylinders were a failure, although some good performances were put up at times, the 'Teutonics' being probably the best. Practically all were withdrawn however as soon as Mr Whale's 'Precursors' began to appear in 1904, although one or two of the 2-2-2-2's lingered on as late as 1912.

During this period much of the important work fell on to the doughty 2-4-0's, of which there were several varieties, some of which were renewals of earlier engines bearing the same name and number. They may be broadly subdivided into three classes, the 'Precedents' with 6' 7½" wheels, the 'Whitworth's' which had smaller 6' 0" wheels, and the 'Precursors' with 5' 6½" wheels. Dealing with the latter first, this consisted of a series of twenty engines, built between 1874 and 1879:—

Number	Name	Number	Name
2145	Precursor	1145	Cossack
2146	Harbinger	1152	Arab
2147	Champion	1153	Sirocco
2148	Vizier	1154	Colossus
2149	Candidate	1155	Dragon
1143	Marquis	402	Viscount
1144	Druid	406	Senator

Number	Name	Number	Name
408	Simoom	1174	Cerberus
409	Thunderbolt	697	Harrowby
413	Python	847	Cedric
425	Oberon	255	Eglinton
426	Warrior	338	Levens
427	Fame	431	Bessemer
1147	John Rennie	481	Etna
1148	Boadicea	626	Emerald
1149	Helvellyn	680	Giffard
1150	Lang Meg	718	Jason
1151	Lapwing	779	William Baker
1165	Vulture	838	Henry Cort
1169	Albatross	1180	Pearl

The 6′ 0″ engines, of which 90 were renewals of older engines, reconstructed between 1889 and 1896, were as follows:—

L.N.W.R. No.	L.M.S. No.	Name
35		Talisman
36		Thalaba
81		Greystoke, (originally Greystock)
124	5090	Marquis Douro
231		Firefly
401		Zeno
404		Zopyrus
418		Zygia
419		Zillah
609	5094	The Earl of Chester
628	5095	Tartarus
632		Ostrich
633		Samson
634	5091	Ellesmere
642	5084	Bee
724		Eden
731		Croxteth
732	5103	Hecla
733	5082	Chimera
735	5088	Charon
736		Memnon
737	5100	Roberts
738		Terrier
739		Sutherland
742		Spitfire
746		Castor

L.N.W.R. No.	L.M.S. No.	Name
748	5080	Waterloo
752		Glowworm
757		Banshee
758		Hardman
763	5092	Violet
764	5093	Shap
792	5099	Theorem
793	5101	Martin
794	5104	Woodlark
795		Falstaff
814	5083	Henrietta
817	5096	Constance
819		Puck
821		Diomede
824	5097	Adelaide
828		Tubal
829		Turk
830		Trent
832		Sanspareil
901	5085	Hero
902		Onyx
934	5089	North Star
935		Planet
1045	5081	Whitworth
90		Luck of Edenhall
209		Petrel
263		Pheasant
285		Phalaris
414		Prospero
424	5107	Sirius
434		St. Patrick
444		Typhon
445		Ixion
446		Siren
468	5086	Wildfire
469		St. George
479		Mastodon
485		Euxine
486	5098	Skiddaw
487		John o'Groat
604	5087	Narcissus
631		Hotspur
635		Zamiel
636		Eclipse
773	5106	Centaur
805		Cyclops/Caliban

L.N.W.R. No.	L.M.S. No.	Name
852		Kestrel
885		Vampire
995		Medea
1162		Saddleback
1163		John of Gaunt
1164		Odin
1166	5108	Wyre
1168	5102	Cuckoo
2150		Atlas
2151		Baltic
2152		Sybil
2153		Isis
2154		Loadstone
2155		Liver
2156		Sphinx
2157	5109	Unicorn
2158	5105	Serpent/Sister Dora
2159		Shark

Finally the 6′ 7½″ engines, the 'Precedents', some of which again were renewals of old engines, were as follows:—

L.N.W.R. No.	L.M.S. No.	Name
271	5004	Minotaur
275		Vulcan
276		Pluto
295		Penmaenmawr
304	5035	Hector
308		Booth
379	5007	Sedgwick
380		Quernmore
381	5037	Patterdale
382		Buckingham
393		Brougham
394		Eamont
395		Scotia
396		Tennyson
403		Isabella
696	5010	Director
787	5038	Clarendon
790	5031	Hardwicke
941	5008	Blenkinsop
942		Shah of Persia
974		Richard Cobden
1020		Wordsworth
1132		North-Western

L.N.W.R. No.	L.M.S. No.	Name
1141		S. R. Graves
1211	5011	John Ramsbottom
1212	5013	Pioneer
1213	5032	The Queen
1214		Prince Albert
1215		Albion
1216		Premier
1217		Florence
1218		Phaeton
1219		Lightning
1220		Belted Will
1480	5009	Newton
1481		The Duke of Edinburgh
1482		Herschel
1483		Newcomen
1484		Telford
1485		Smeaton
1486		Dalton
1487		Faraday
1488	5014	Murdock
1489		Brindley
1513		Shakespeare
1514		Scott
1515		Milton
1516		Byron
1517		Princess Helena
1518	5025	Countess
1519	5026	Duchess
1520	5027	Franklin
1521	5017	Gladstone
1522	5005	Pitt
1523		Marlborough
1524		Wolfe
1525	5022	Abercrombie
1526		Drake
1527	5006	Raleigh
1528		Frobisher
1529		Cook
1530		Columbus
1531	5019	Cromwell
1532		Hampden
1666	5028	Ariadne
1667	5039	Corunna
1668	5023	Dagmar
1669		Ilion
1670		Ganymede

L.N.W.R. No.	L.M.S. No.	Name
1671		Shamrock
1672	5018	Talavera
1673		Lucknow
1674	5020	Delhi
1675	5024	Vimiera
1676		The Nile
1677		Badajos
1678	5033	Airey
1679		Bunsen
1680		Livingstone
1681		Minerva
1682	5036	Novelty
1683		Sisyphus
1684	5029	Speke
1685	5015	Gladiator
1744		Magdala
1745	5034	John Bright/Glowworm
1746		Bevere
1747		John Mayall
1748	5016	Britannia
1749		Hibernia
2001		Henry Crosfield
2002	5030	Madge
2003		Alecto
2004		Witch
2005	5041	Lynx
2006	5021	Princess
2175		Precedent
2176	5061	Robert Benson
2177		Edward Tootal
2178		Pluck
2179		Patience
2180	5073	Perseverence
2181		Buffalo
2182		Giraffe
2183	5054	Antelope
2184		Reynard
2185	5058	Alma
2186	5067	Lowther
2187	5069	Penrith Beacon
2188		Chillington
2189	5076	Avon
2190	5000	Princess Beatrice
2191	5001	Snowdon
2192	5043	Caradoc
2193	5059	Salopian

Highland Railway—4-6-0 Dunrobin Castle.

Highland Railway. Drummond 0-4-4T.

Highland Railway. One of the only three engines built by William Stroudley during his short term
of office before going to the L.B. & S.C.R.

Highland Railway — 4-4-0 'Glentruim', in early L.M.S. days.

[L. R. Tomsett

Highland 'Large Ben' No. 14418, 'Ben Mheadhoin' also in early L.M.S. days.

Two styles of lettering as used on Highland engines after the grouping.

'The Prince'—the only L.M.S. built tank engine to carry a name.

Royal Scot' No. 6148 as subsequently renamed.

L.M.S.R. 'Jubilee' No. 5719.

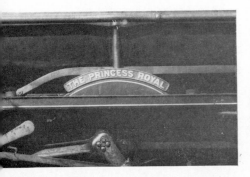

L.M.S.R. 'Princess' class Pacific No. 6200.

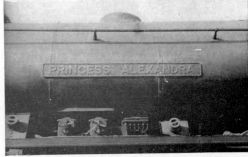

L.M.S.R. 'Coronation' class Pacific No. 6224.

L.M.S.R. 'The Royal Scot' after its return from its tour in the U.S.A. The inset shows the commemorative plaque, and rather unusually the name was also displayed on the smokebox door in place of the usual number plate. This was carried until its rebuild with taper boiler in 1950.

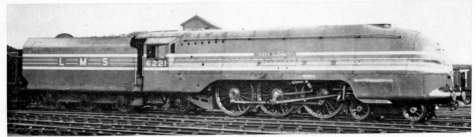

[W. Leslie Good

L.M.S.R. streamlined Pacific 'Queen Elizabeth' as originally built.

L.M.S.R. 'City of Glasgow' as subsequently de-streamlined.

L.N.W.R. No.	L.M.S. No.	Name
2194	5066	Cambrian
857	5074	Prince Leopold
858		Sir Salar Jung
860	5050	Merrie Carlisle
861	5079	Amazon
862	5075	Balmoral
863		Meteor
864	5063	Pilot
865	5046	Envoy
866	5057	Courier
867		Disraeli
868		Condor
869		Llewellyn
870	5078	Fairbairn
871	5044	Proserpine
872		Wizard
883	5049	Phantom
890	5051	Sir Hardman Earle
1105	5077	Hercules
1177		Princess Louise
1189		Stewart
193	5072	Rocket
517		Marathon
749	5052	Mercury
919	5040	Nasmyth
1170	5002	General
1173	5042	The Auditor
1183		Plynlimmon
1187	5064	Chandos
1193		Joshua Radcliffe
1194	5068	Miranda
619	5060	Mabel
789		Breadalbane
477	5056	Caractacus
478	5065	Commodore
480	5071	Duchess of Lancaster
482		Pegasus
506	5062	Sir Alexander Cockburn
512	5003	Lazonby
514		Lawrence
945	5053	Humphry Davy
253	5047	President Garfield
254		President Lincoln
256		President Washington
257		Duke of Albany
260		Duke of Connaught

L.N.W.R. No.	L.M.S. No.	Name
262	5070	Wheatstone
264		Buckland
265	5045	Thomas Carlyle
364	5048	Henry Pease
955		Charles Dickens

Of the 110 engines of the 'Whitworth' and 'Precedent' class which lasted into L.M.S. days, not all survived actually to carry the new allotted numbers as shown in the above table. The last in service was No. 5001 'Snowdon', which was again renumbered 25001 and was withdrawn in 1934.

'Hardwicke' was retained for preservation, duly restored to L.N.W.R. livery, and after a sojourn of thirty years in Crewe paint shop has now taken up its final abode in Clapham Museum.

4-4-0 COMPOUNDS. 'JUBILEE' CLASS BUILT 1897-1900

L.N.W.R. No.	L.M.S. No.	Name
1901	5156	Jubilee
1902	5157	Black Prince
1903	5110	Iron Duke
1904	5111	Rob Roy
1905	5137	Black Diamond
1906	5149	Robin Hood
1907	5178	Black Watch
1908		Royal George
1909	5159	Crusader
1910	5172	Cavalier
1911	5112	Centurion
1912	5113	Colossus
1913	5132	Canopus
1914	5144	Invincible
1915	5114	Implacable
1916	5155	Irresistible
1917	5184	Inflexible
1918	5131	Renown
1919	5160	Resolution
1920	5166	Flying Fox
1921	5134	T. H. Ismay/John of Gaunt
1922	5146	Intrepid
1923	5115	Agamemnon
1924	5183	Powerful
1925	5147	Warrior
1926	5180	La France
1927	5116	Goliath
1928	5173	Glatton

L.N.W.R. No.	L.M.S. No.	Name
1929	5117	Polyphemus
1930	5142	Ramillies
1931	5176	Agincourt
1932	5162	Anson
1933	5169	Barfleur
1934	5165	Blenheim
1935	5133	Collingwood
1936	5150	Royal Sovereign
1937	5154	Superb
1938	5161	Sultan
1939	5158	Temeraire
1940	5170	Trafalgar

No. 1914 was renumbered 1257 in 1920, when it was desired to give the number 1914 to a new engine, 'Patriot' as a memorial to the first world war.

4-4-0 COMPOUNDS. 'ALFRED THE GREAT' CLASS

L.N.W.R. No.	L.M.S. No.	Name
1941	5179	Alfred the Great
1942	5185	King Edward VII
1943	5145	Queen Alexandra
1944	5118	Victoria and Albert
1945	5139	Magnificent
1946	5138	Diadem
1947	5174	Australia
1948	5141	Camperdown
1949	5152	King Arthur
1950	5186	Victorious
1951	5136	Bacchante
1952	5119	Benbow
1953	5120	Formidable
1954	5121	Galatea
1955	5122	Hannibal
1956		Illustrious
1957	5148	Orion
1958	5181	Royal Oak
1959	5143	Revenge
1960	5153	Francis Stevenson
1961	5140	Albermarle/Albemarle
1962	5171	Aurora
1963	5163	Boadicea
1964	5123	Caesar
1965	5151	Charles H. Mason
1966	5124	Commonwealth

L.N.W.R. No.	*L.M.S. No.*	*Name*
1967	5125	Cressy
1968	5164	Cumberland
1969	5126	Dominion
1970	5127	Good Hope
1971	5135	Euryalus
1972	5168	Hindostan
1973	5175	Hood
1974	5128	Howe
1975	5167	Jupiter
1976		Lady Godiva
1977	5129	Mars
1978	5177	Merlin
1979	5130	Nelson
1980	5182	Neptune

From 1908 onwards a large number of both 'Jubilees' and 'Alfred the Great' class were rebuilt as simple engines with two inside cylinders. The last engine to run as a compound was No. 1974 'Howe' (allocated L.M.S. No. 5128 but never carried), withdrawn in 1928. Some of the rebuilt engines lasted until 1931.

These can be distinguished in the above table by being those allocated numbers 5131 and upwards by the L.M.S.

Nos. 1908, 1956 and 1976 were scrapped prior to the grouping.

4-4-0's 'PRECURSOR' CLASS

Mr Whale's first passenger class, introduced in 1904, which were an immediate success, fulfilled a long felt want in supplying a good, reliable and powerful engine for the heavy express work on the L.N.W.R. main line.

No less than 130 were built between 1904 and 1907. Many were later fitted with superheaters, and when the L.M.S. renumbering scheme was drawn up in 1923 the unsuperheated and superheated engines were segregated, the former becoming 5187-5266 and the latter 5270-5319, although subsequently in several cases non-superheated engines received superheaters, and vice versa.

For convenience, the engines are listed in L.M.S. number order:—

L.N.W.R. No.	*L.M.S. No.*	*Name*
2023	5187	Helvellyn
412	5188	Alfred Paget/Marquis
510	5189	Albatross
639	5190	Ajax
648	5191	Archimedes
685	5192	Cossack
1102	5193	Thunderbolt

L.N.W.R. No.	L.M.S. No.	Name
1117	5194	Vandal
622	5195	Euphrates
638	5196	Huskisson
645	5197	Mammoth
408	5198	Niagara
1104	5199	Cedric
1111	5200	Cerberus
1431	5201	Egeria
520	5202	Panopea
2031	5203	Waverley
184	5204	Havelock
1115	5205	Apollo
1545	5206	Cyclops
2061	5207	Eglinton
519	5208	Messenger
2120	5209	Trentham
1430	5210	Victor
113	5211	Aurania
315	5212	Harrowby
311	5213	Emperor
1509	5214	America
2257	5215	Vulture
911	5216	Herald
1114	5217	Knowsley
1116	5218	Pandora
1510	5219	Psyche
1784	5229	Python
2202	5221	Vizier
117	5222	Alaska
127	5223	Snake
229	5224	Stork
1301	5225	Candidate
1396	5226	Harpy
2007	5227	Oregon
2012	5228	Penguin
2115	5229	Servia
2576	5230	Arab
2579	5231	Ganymede
2580	5232	Problem
2581	5233	Peel
2582	5234	Rowland Hill
2583	5235	Moonstone
2585	5236	Watt
234	5237	Pearl
526	5238	Ilion
723	5239	Coptic

L.N.W.R. No.	L.M.S. No.	Name
837	5240	Friar
1311	5241	Napoleon
1312	5242	Ionic
1642	5243	Lapwing
2017	5244	Tubal
561	5245	Antaeus
675	5246	Adjutant
772	5247	Admiral
804	5248	Amphion
988	5249	Bellerophon
1433	5250	Faerie Queene
1650	5251	Richard Trevithick
1787	5252	Hyperion
1	5253	Clive
218	5254	Daphne
419	5255	Monarch
665	5256	Mersey
1011	5257	Locke
1364	5258	Clyde
2053	5259	Edith
2181	5260	Eleanor
276	5261	Doric
754	5262	Celtic
807	5263	Oceanic
976	5264	Pacific
1297	5265	Phalaris
1516	5266	Alecto
469	5270	Marmion
802	5271	Gaelic
1363	5272	Brindley
2064	5273	Jason
688	5274	Hecate
1439	5275	Tiger
7	5276	Titan
2164	5277	Oberon
513	5278	Precursor
2062	5279	Sunbeam
2166	5280	Shooting Star
564	5281	Erebus
515	5282	Champion
2011	5283	Brougham
333	5284	Ambassador
1419	5285	Tamerlane
1573	5286	Dunrobin
365	5287	Alchymist
1469	5288	Tantalus

L.N.W.R. No.	L.M.S. No.	Name
301	5289	Leviathan
310	5290	Achilles
1395	5291	Harbinger
366	5292	Medusa
2513	5293	Levens
106	5294	Druid
1723	5295	Scorpion
659	5296	Dreadnought
643	5297	Sirocco
60	5298	Dragon
1137	5299	Vesuvius
1617	5300	Hydra
300	5301	Emerald
1309	5302	Shamrock
323	5303	Argus
302	5304	Greyhound
303	5305	Himalaya
1387	5306	Lang Meg
305	5307	Senator
2	5308	Simoom
2578	5309	Fame
1120	5310	Thunderer
811	5311	Express
2584	5312	Velocipede
2577	5313	Etna
282	5314	Alaric
2051	5315	Delamere
1737	5316	Viscount
374	5317	Empress
806	5318	Swiftsure
990	5319	Bucephalus

Withdrawal began in 1927 and in 1934 the thirty one survivors were again renumbered by the addition of 20000, becoming 25187 etc.

No. 25297 'Sirocco' was the last survivor, and lasted till Nationalisation days, being allotted B.R. No. 58010 in 1948, which it never carried, being scrapped in the same year.

4-4-0 'GEORGE V' CLASS

Superheated development of the 'Precursor' class, ninety engines built between 1910 and 1915.

L.N.W.R. No.	L.M.S. No.	Name
2663	5320	George the Fifth
1059	5321	Lord Loch
1294	5322	F. S. P. Wolferstan

L.N.W.R. No.	*L.M.S. No.*	*Name*
1583	5323	Henry Ward
1725	5324	John Bateson
2025	5325	Sir Thomas Brooke
2155	5326	W. C. Brocklehurst
228	5327	E. Nettlefold
445	5328	P. H. Chambres
2664	5329	Queen Mary
1550	5330	Westminster
2271	5331	J. P. Bickersteth
896	5332	George Whale
1559	5333	Drake
2151	5334	Newcomen
2507	5335	Miles MacInnes
238	5336	F. W. Webb
1195	5337	T. J. Hare
2512	5338	Thomas Houghton
2168	5339	Henry Maudslay
956	5340	Bulldog
1489	5341	Wolfhound
1504	5342	Boarhound
1513	5343	Otterhound
1532	5344	Bloodhound
1628	5345	Foxhound
1662	5346	Deerhound
1706	5347	Elkhound
1800/5000	5348	Coronation
502	5349	British Empire
868	5350	India
882	5351	Canada
1218	5352	Australia
1792	5353	Staghound
2081	5354	New Zealand
2212	5355	South Africa
2291	5356	Gibraltar
2495	5357	Bassethound
2177	5358	Malta
2498	5359	Cyprus
361	5360	Beagle
888	5361	Challenger
1360	5362	Fire Queen
1394	5363	Harrier
1623	5364	Nubian
1631	5365	Racehorse
1644	5366	Roebuck
2089	5367	Traveller
2494	5368	Perseus

L.N.W.R. No.	L.M.S. No.	Name
1371	5369	Quail
1417	5370	Landrail
1472	5371	Moor Hen
1595	5372	Wild Duck
1681	5373	Ptarmigan
2220	5374	Vanguard
1713	5357	Partridge
1730	5376	Snipe
1733	5377	Grouse
1777	5378	Widgeon
1799	5379	Woodcock
82	5380	Charles Dickens
752	5381	John Hick
2124	5382	John Rennie
89	5383	John Mayall
132	5384	S. R. Graves
1138	5385	William Froude
1193	5386	Edward Tootal
2154	5387	William Siemens
2282	5388	Richard Arkwright
404	5389	Eclipse
681	5390	St. George
845	5391	Saddleback
1188	5392	Penmaenmawr
1680	5393	Loyalty
2086	5394	Phaeton
2279	5395	Henry Crosfield
1481	5396	Typhon
2197	5397	Planet
2242	5398	Meteor
2428	5399	Lord Stalbridge
363	5400	Llandudno
789	5401	Windermere
984	5402	Carnarvon
104	5403	Leamington Spa
226	5404	Colwyn Bay
1086	5405	Conway
2153	5406	Llandrindod
2233	5407	Blackpool
2106	5408	Holyhead
2370	5409	Dovedale

Thirty seven engines were still in existence in 1934 and had 20000 added to their numbers. By 1948 two remained, Nos. 25350 (name latterly removed) and 25373 'Ptarmigan' and although allotted B.R. Nos. 58011/2 did not survive to carry them.

4-6-0 'EXPERIMENT' CLASS

Shortly after the introduction of the 4-4-0 'Precursors', Mr Whale introduced a 4-6-0 engine with 6' 3" wheels for express work on the more hilly sections of the main line north of Crewe. 105 engines were built between 1905 and 1910.

L.N.W.R. No.	*L.M.S. No.*	*Name*
66	5450	Experiment
306	5451	Autocrat
353	5452	Britannic
372	5453	Germanic/Belgic
507	5454	Sarmatian
565	5455	City of Carlisle
893	5456	City of Chester
1074	5457	City of Dublin
1357	5458	City of Edinburgh
165	5459	City of Lichfield
828	5460	City of Liverpool
978	5461	City of London
1405	5462	City of Manchester
1575	5463	City of Paris
1669	5464	City of Glasgow
1986	5465	Clanricarde
1987	5466	Glendower
1988	5467	Hurricane
1989	5468	Lady of the Lake
1990	5469	North Western
1991	5470	Palmerston
1992	5471	President
1993	5472	Richard Moon
1994	5473	Scottish Chief
61	5474	Atalanta
222	5475	Ivanhoe
291	5476	Leander
667	5477	Mazeppa
1304	5478	Prometheus
1676	5479	Prince of Wales/ Shakespeare
1709	5480	Princess May
1995	5481	Tornado
2027	5482	Queen Empress
2052	5483	Stephenson
2269	5484	William Cawkwell
496	5485	Harlequin
830	5486	Phosphorus
902	5487	Combermere

L.N.W.R. No.	L.M.S. No.	Name
937	5488	Princess Alice
1014	5489	Henry Bessemer
2112	5490	Victoria
1135	5491	Prince George
1526	5492	Sanspareil
2161	5493	Jeanie Deans
322	5494	Adriatic
884	5495	Greater Britain
887	5496	Fortuna
1020	5497	Majestic
1483	5498	Red Gauntlet
1490	5499	Wellington
1553	5500	Faraday
1571	5501	Herschel
2076	5502	Pheasant
2116	5503	Greystoke
2621	5504	Ethelred
2622	5505	Eunomia
2623	5506	Lord of the Isles
2624	5507	Saracen
2625	5508	Buckland
2626	5509	Chillington
2627	5510	President Lincoln
2628	5511	Banshee
2629	5512	Terrier
2630	5513	Buffalo
1406	5514	George Findlay
1413	5515	Henry Cort
1477	5516	Hugh Myddleton
1498	5517	Thomas Savery
1566	5518	John Penn
1603	5519	Princess Alexandra
1649	5520	Sisyphus
1661	5521	Wordsworth
1781	5522	Lightning
2022	5523	Marlborough
2637	5524	Babylon
2638	5525	Byzantium
2639	5526	Bactria
2640	5527	Belisarius
2641	5528	Bellona
2642	5529	Berenice
2643	5530	Bacchus
2644	5531	Berengaria
2645	5532	Britomart
2646	5533	Boniface

L.N.W.R. No.	L.M.S. No.	Name
1412	5534	Bedfordshire
1418	5535	Cheshire
1420	5536	Derbyshire
1455	5537	Herefordshire
1611	5538	Hertfordshire
1616	5539	Lancashire
71	5540	Oxfordshire
275	5541	Shropshire
677	5542	Staffordshire
1002	5543	Warwickshire
1534	5544	Westmorland
1624	5545	Leicestershire
1652	5546	Middlesex
1689	5547	Monmouthshire
1703	5548	Northumberland
1471	5549	Worcestershire
1561	5550	Yorkshire
1618	5551	Carnarvonshire
1621	5552	Denbighshire
1658	5553	Flintshire
1361	5554	Prospero

Scrapping began in 1928 and not all of them survived actually to carry their allotted L.M.S. numbers. A few lasted until 1934 however, to be re-numbered into the 20000 series, and the last in service was No. 25473 'Scottish Chief', scrapped in 1935.

The only ones to be superheated were Nos. 1993 'Richard Moon' and No. 1361 'Prospero' which was rebuilt at the same time as a 4 cylinder engine.

4-6-0 'PRINCE OF WALES' CLASS

Superheated development of the 'Experiment' class, 245 engines built between 1911 and 1921. Many of the last built ones however never received names, and only those that did are tabulated in the following list:—

L.N.W.R. No.	L.M.S. No.	Name
819	5600	Prince of Wales
1388	5601	Andromeda
1452	5602	Bonaventure
1454	5603	Coquette
1537	5604	Enchantress
1691	5605	Pathfinder
1704	5606	Conqueror
1721	5607	Defiance
2021	5608	Wolverine
2359	5609	Hermione
362	5610	Robert Southey
892	5611	Charles Wolfe

L.N.W.R. No.	L.M.S. No.	Name
1081	5612	John Keats
1089	5613	Sydney Smith
1134	5614	Victor Hugo
2040	5615	Oliver Goldsmith
2075	5616	Robert Burns
321	5617	Henry W. Longfellow
479	5618	Thomas B. Macaulay
951	5619	Bulwer Lytton
2198	5629	John Ruskin
2205	5621	Thomas Moore
2213	5622	Charles Kingsley
1679	5623	Lord Byron
2249	5624	Thomas Campbell
2283	5625	Robert L. Stevenson
86	5626	Mark Twain
146	5627	Lewis Carroll
307	5628	R. B. Sheridan
637	5629	Thomas Gray
979	5630	W. M. Thackeray
1400	5631	Felicia Hemans
694	5632	Bret Harte
985	5633	Sir W. S. Gilbert
1321	5634	William Cowper
2152	5635	Charles Lamb
2293	5636	Percy Bysshe Shelley
2377	5637	Edward Gibbon
2443	5638	Charles James Lever
2520	5639	G. P. Neele
27	5640	General Joffre
88	5641	Czar of Russia
122	5642	King of the Belgians
160	5643	King of Serbia
185	5644	King of Italy
877	5645	Raymond Poincare
1333	5646	Sir John French
2275	5647	Edith Cavell
2396	5648	Queen of the Belgians
2408	5649	Admiral Jellicoe
606	5650	Castor
745	5651	Pluto
810	5652	Onyx
1352	5653	The Nile
1379	5654	Witch
1484	5655	Smeaton
1084	5656	Shark
1346	5657	Trent

L.N.W.R. No.	*L.M.S. No.*	*Name*
2417	5658	Atlas
2442	5659	Odin
90	5660	Kestrel
95	5661	Gallipoli
126	5662	Anzac
136	5663	Minerva
173	5664	Livingstone
233	5665	Suvla Bay
257	5666	Plynlimmon
401	5667	Zamiel
446	5668	Pegasus
525	5669	Vulcan
610	5670	Albion
849	5671	Arethusa
867	5672	Condor
1100	5673	Lusitania
1132	5674	Scott
1466	5675	Sphinx
1744	5676	Petrel
1749	5677	Precedent
2055	5678	Milton
2063	5679	Hibernia
2175	5680	Loadstone
2203	5681	Falstaff
2339	5682	Samson
1324	5683	Falaba
2092	5684	Arabic
2276	5685	Persia
2295	5686	Anglia
2300	5687	Hotspur
2340	5688	Tara
2392	5689	Caliban
940	5697	Richard Cobden
621	5700	Telford
1584	5704	Scotia
504	5706	Canning
974	5707	Hampden
522	5723	Stentor
1290	5729	Lucknow
1325	5736	Disraeli
1178	5743	Prince Albert
1542	5750	Marathon
1694	5753	Premier
2516	5754	Dalton

The majority of these engines were renumbered by the addition of 20000 in 1934, although a few, including the original 'Prince of Wales' which consequently never became 25600, had been scrapped by that time. Survivors in 1948 were No. 25648 'Queen of the Belgians', 25673 'Lusitania' and also an unnamed one, No. 25752, but although these were allocated B. R. Nos. 58000–58002 they did not live long enough to carry them.

The name 'Prince of Wales' reappeared once more on a new engine built in 1924 to a modified 'Prince of Wales' design embodying outside Walschaert valve gear (four engines of the original series already having been so converted). Although not strictly a L.N.W.R. engine, it can best be included here as it was the last engine to be built of L.N.W.R. design. It was numbered 5845, and bore the name 'Prince of Wales' for a short time only whilst on view at Wembley Exhibition. It became No. 25845 in 1934 and was scrapped in 1947.

'CLAUGHTON' CLASS 4 CYLINDER 4-6-0's

The last express design for the L.N.W.R. 130 engines built between 1913 and 1921, but like the 'Princes' most of the later ones never received names.

L.N.W.R. No.	L.M.S. No.	Name
2222	5900	Sir Gilbert Claughton
1161	5901	Sir Robert Turnbull
1191	5902	Sir Frank Ree
21	5903	Duke of Sutherland
163	5094	Holland Hibbert
650	5905	Lord Rathmore
1159	5906	Ralph Brocklebank
1319	5907	Sir Frederick Harrison
1327	5908	Alfred Fletcher
2046	5909	Charles N. Lawrence
250	5910	J. A. Bright
260	5911	W. E. Dorrington
1131	5912	Lord Faber
1429	5913	Colonel Lockwood
209	5914	J. Bruce Ismay
668	5915	Rupert Guinness
856	5916	E. Tootal Broadhurst
1567	5917	Charles J. Cropper
2239	5918	Frederick Baynes
2401	5919	Lord Kitchener
511	5920	George Macpherson
695	5921	Sir Arthur Lawley
968	5922	Lord Kenyon
1093	5923	Guy Calthrop/Sir Guy Calthrop
1345	5924	James Bishop
2174	5925	E. C. Trench
2204	5926	Sir Herbert Walker/Sir Herbert Walker K.C.B.
2221	5927	Sir Francis Dent

L.N.W.R. No.	*L.M.S. No.*	*Name*
2338	5928	Charles H. Dent
2395	5929	J. A. F. Aspinall
37	5930	G. R. Jebb
154	5931	Captain Fryatt
155	5932	I. T. Williams/Sir Thomas Williams
2230	5939	Clio
1019	5940	Columbus
2373	5943	Tennyson
2420	5945	Ingestre
2427	5946	Duke of Connaught
2445	5948	Baltic
986	5953	Buckingham
1914	5964	Patriot*
1177	5966	Bunsen
1407	5967	Lance Corporal J. A. Christie, v.c.
1599	5968	John o' Groat
2499	5970	Patience
2511	5971	Croxteth
12	5975	Talisman
2035	5976	Private E. Sykes, v.c.
2268	5979	Frobisher
1097	5988	Private W. Wood, v.c.
2059	5991	C. J. Bowen Cooke
2430	5999	Vindictive
30	6002	Thalaba
42	6004	Princess Louise
110	6008	Lady Godiva
150	6011	Illustrious
158	6015	Private E. Sykes, v.c.
169	6017	Breadalbane
179	6018	Private W. Wood, v.c.
180	6019	Llewellyn
192	6021	Bevere
207	6023	Sir Charles Cust

* The L.N.W.R. War Memorial engine. The plate also bore the words 'In memory of the fallen L.N.W.R. employees, 1914–1919'.

Most of the class disappeared during the 1930's, but three of the named engines, Nos. 5946, 6017 and 6023 remained at work until 1940–1. The last survivor of all was No. 6004, whose name had been removed in 1936, which lasted until 1949, having outlived all of its sisters by several years.

There only remains to be enumerated the very small number of tank engines of the North Western to bear names. These were incidentally the only instances of a departure from its standard style of brass nameplate with

[*W. H. Whitworth*

Seven examples of the nameplates as applied to the L.M.S.R. 'Royal Scots' 6125-6149 when first built.
The eighth illustration shows the plate applied to the rebuilt N.6170.

Great Eastern Railway 'Claud Hamilton' as built.

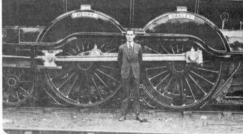

The new plate as applied by Gresley to the rebuilt 'Claud Hamilton'.

Great Northern Railway Atlantic No. 990.

North Eastern Railway 'Aerolite'.

One of the four **G.C.R.** compound Atlantics, all of which bore names.

Of Robinson's **G.C.R.** D9 4-4-0's, only four ever carried names. This view shows one of them in the later rebuilt condition and with its appearance much ruined by the ugly chimney and cut-down dome.

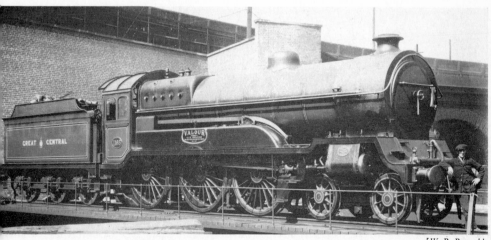

The Great Central War Memorial engine.

One of the twenty-four Robinson 'Director' engines, built in 1924 for working in Scotland, shown in its original condition.

The original G.N.R. Pacific as rebuilt by Mr. Thompson in 1945 and painted experimentally in G.E.R. R. Blue livery.

The nameplate later fitted to 'Great Northern' of smaller design than that shown in the preceding picture and surmounted by the crest of the former Company.

Nameplate on G.C.R. 4-6-0 No. 1097

sunken lettering. In this case the plate was somewhat larger with raised lettering more after the style of the Great Western.

The engines concerned belonged to the numerous class of 0-6-0ST's built by Mr Webb during the 1870's and generally known as 'Special tanks'. One of them, originally 2359, was transferred to Earlestown Wagon works for departmental duties, whereupon it appropriately received the name 'Earlestown'. In more recent years it joined three others of the class (unnamed) on shunting duties at Wolverton Carriage works, where it was in service until 1957. It retained its name until the end.

Two other engines of the class which had been rebuilt with square shaped saddletanks, Nos. 3021 and 3186, were named respectively 'Liverpool' and 'Euston', and were used principally on working boat trains between Edge Hill and the Riverside at Liverpool, although in 1924 'Euston' was acting as shed pilot at Camden. This one was scrapped in 1928, but 'Liverpool', as L.M.S. No. 27334, lasted until 1939.

Finally there were the diminutive narrow gauge engines which worked on the one time extensive narrow gauge system at Crewe Works. This was abandoned in the early 1930's.

The engines, which were unnumbered, were known as 'Billy', 'Dickie', 'Midge', 'Nipper', 'Pet', 'Tiny', and 'Topsy'. 'Pet' has been preserved. All of these had standard L.N.W.R. nameplates of the same design as used on the main line engines.

Latterly there was also a Diesel engine, 'Crewe', bearing the No. 5519, probably a maker's number as it was not a Crewe built product.

There were also three other narrow gauge engines used by the Engineering Department at Crewe, two 0-4-0ST's named 'Platelayer' and 'Kitchener' and a 0-4-2ST 'Jim Crow', all of quite different design. They were unnumbered.

These engines were very little known and disappeared during the Second World War.

Lancashire and Yorkshire Railway

The L. & Y. R. had no named main line engines since earlier days, but like the North Western it had a few on the narrow gauge system at Horwich works similar to L.N.W.R. one at Crewe just mentioned. The tiny engines which worked on this lay-out, formerly eight in number, carried small nameplates on the unusual position of the safety valve cover. These were 'Midget', 'Mouse', 'Robin', 'Wasp', 'Wren', 'Dot', 'Fly', and 'Bee', but for many years latterly the small amount of narrow gauge line still in use provided work for only one engine, for which purpose 'Wren' (assisted by a small diesel) had been retained. It is now preserved in Clapham Museum.

Midland Railway

Throughout its whole existence, from its formation in 1844 by amalgamation of the Midland Counties, Birmingham and Derby Junction, and North Midland Railways, down to its absorption into the London, Midland and

Scottish in 1923, the Midland Railway bestowed names on but two of its locomotives.

The first of these was on one of Mr Johnson's numerous series of 4-4-0 express engines, built in 1887, No. 1757, which was given the name 'Beatrice' on a brass plate carried in the customary position on the leading splasher. She was shown at an exhibition near Bradford in the year in which she was built. For a number of years the engine worked through trains between St. Pancras and Shoeburyness on the L.T. & S.R. system (which line was eventually absorbed in 1912 by the Midland).

'Beatrice' was rebuilt with a larger boiler in 1907, at the same time was renumbered 377 and lost her name. She was again rebuilt with superheater in 1923, eventually becoming B.R. No. 40377 and being finally withdrawn from service in 1955.

The other Midland engine to receive a name was the first of the final batch of ten of Mr Johnson's magnificent single wheelers, regarded by many as the loveliest engines ever designed. No. 2601, 'Princess of Wales' appeared from Derby works in 1900 and was exhibited at the Paris exhibition of that year. She did fine work on the southern part of the Midland main line for about twenty years, being stationed at Kentish Town for her whole existence. Her comparatively short life was occasioned, not by any defect in the design, but by the increasing weight of the trains which put the single wheeler at a considerable disadvantage.

The name in this case was painted on the splasher, and under the 1907 re-numbering scheme she became No. 685. She was withdrawn from service in 1920 and lay at Kentish Town for a year more afterwards, when she was taken to Derby for scrap. Her driving wheels were preserved there for a number of years, but eventually disappeared.

London Tilbury and Southend Railway

When the L.T. & S.R. was absorbed by the Midland in 1912 no less than eighty out of the total of 82 locomotives were named. The two exceptions were a couple of 0-6-0 tender engines, all the rest of its stock consisting of tanks, mostly of the 4-4-2T type together with a few 0-6-2T's. The names were painted on the tank sides in semi circular fashion, surmounting the Company's coat of arms. At the time of the absorption four further 0-6-2T's were on order together with eight massive 4-6-4T's of a new design, but although it was intended that all of these should be named the Midland had other ideas on the matter, and not only did the new engines appear nameless, but as the older engines went through the shops and were repainted in Midland red they also were denamed.

The 4-4-2T's, which were of three classes, built as follows:—

L.T.S. No.	Name	L.T.S. No.	Name
1	Southend	5	Plaistow
2	Gravesend	6	Upton Park
3	Tilbury	7	Barking
4	Bromley	8	Rainham

L.T.S. No.	Name	L.T.S. No.	Name
9	Purfleet/Tilbury Docks	41	Leytonstone
		42	Commercial Road/
10	Grays		East Horndon
11	Stanford	43	Great Ilford
12	Pitsea	44	Prittlewell
13	Benfleet/Black Horse Road	45	Shoeburyness
		46	Southchurch
14	Leigh	47	Stratford
15	East Ham	48	Little Ilford
16	Low Street	51	Tilbury Docks/
17	Thames-Haven		Purfleet
18	Burdett Road	52	Wennington
19	Dagenham	53	Stepney Green
20	Hornchurch	54	Mile End
21	Upminster	55	Wellington Road/
22	East Horndon/ Commercial Road		Bow Road
		56	Harringay
23	Laindon	57	Crouch Hill
24	Ockendon	58	Hornsey Road/
25	Stifford		Hornsey
26	West Thurrock	59	Holloway Road/
27	Whitechapel		Holloway
28	Romford	60	Highgate
29	Stepney	61	Kentish Town
30	Fenchurch	62	Camden Road/
31	St. Pancras		Camden
32	Leyton	63	Mansion House
33	Wanstead	64	Charing Cross
34	Tottenham	65	Victoria
35	West Ham	66	Earl's Court
36	Walthamstow	67	Westminster
37	Woodgrange	68	Mark Lane
38	Westcliff	79	Rippleside
39	Forest Gate	80	Thundersley*
40	Black Horse Road/ Benfleet	81	Aveley
		82	Crowstone

The 0-6-2T's which had come out in 1903 and 1908, were as follows:—

L.T.S. No.	Name	L.T.S. No.	Name
69	Corringham	74	Orsett
70	Basildon	75	Canvey Island
71	Wakering	76	Dunton
72	Hadleigh	77	Fobbing
73	Cranham	78	Dagenham Dock

* Temporarily named "Southend-on-Sea" when on exhibition at White City in 1909; this engine has been preserved, repainted in L.T.S. livery with name restored.

The Midland at first renumbered the L.T. & S.R. tank engines between 2100 and 2193, but later sundry renumberings took place on the construction of further 4-4-2T's to the same design as the later Tilbury engines proper. The smallest class, which had been Nos. 1–36 on the L.T. & S.R., were scrapped by the L.M.S. in the 1930's. What may be called the 'Intermediates' old Nos. 51-68, nearly all lasted into B.R. days, and were taken out of service between 1947 and 1953, the last to go being No. 63, which finished up as B.R. 41922, all of the surviving L.T. & S.R. engines being latterly numbered in the 41900's. The remainder, old 37–48 and 79–82, all went during 1951 and 1952, but No. 80 'Thundersley' has been restored to its L.T. & S.R. livery and preserved.

The 0-6-2T's, which had become B.R. 41980–41993, lasted until 1958/9 with the exception of No. 41981 (old 70) which was not finally withdrawn until 1962, and although it had done little or no work during its final year or two, was the last L.T. & S.R. engine to remain in the stock list.

North Staffordshire Railway

Only two main line engines of the N.S.R. received names, these being two 2-4-0's built in 1882

54   John Bramley Moore   55   Colin Minton Campbell

They were scrapped in 1920 and 1911 respectively.

The last N.S.R. engine to remain in service under L.M.S. auspices was taken out of service as long ago as 1939—along with the Glasgow and South Western this was one of the first of the pre-grouping locomotive stock to be eliminated—but mention should be made of five of its comparatively modern 0-6-2T's, two of them built in 1923, which were sold to the Walkden Colliery, Manchester (now part of the National Coal Board) and which in 1962 were still at work. The coal company had named them as follows:—

N.S.R. No.	L.M.S. No.	Name (as supplied by Colliery)
1	2270	Queen Elizabeth
2	2271	Princess
22	2264	Kenneth
69	2257	King George VI
72	2262	Sir Robert

The names were placed on the bunker, a somewhat unusual position, but in 1960 'Princess' was repainted in its original N.S.R. livery in connection with the Centenary celebrations and lost its newly acquired name in consequence. Another of the class was sold to the War Department.

For working the 3′ 6″ gauge system at Caldon Low Quarries three 0-4-0ST's were obtained in 1887 and 1890. They were not numbered in the ordinary locomotive stock, but were named 'Bobs', 'Frog', and 'Toad'. They were scrapped when the quarries closed in the 1930's.

Leek and Manifold Valley Light Railway

This picturesque narrow gauge line, although nominally independent, was in fact worked by the N.S.R., and was in practice a subsidiary of that Company. In consequence it came into the hands of the L.M.S. at the grouping.

There were two locomotives, 2-6-4T's built by Kitson's in 1904:—

No. 1   E. R. Calthrop   No. 2   J. B. Earle

They were never renumbered by the L.M.S. and were scrapped after the closure of the line in 1935.

Garstang and Knott End Railway

This railway had four locomotives. It was absorbed into the L.M.S. at the grouping.

L.M.S. No.	Name	Type	Withdrawn
11300	Jubilee Queen	0-6-0ST	1926
(11301)*	New Century	,,	1925
(11302)*	Knott End	0-6-0T	1924
11680	Blackpool	2-6-0T	1927

* The L.M.S. numbers were never actually carried.

Cleator and Workington Railway

Five locomotives. Absorbed into L.M.S. at the grouping.

C. & W. No.	L.M.S. No.	Name	Type	Withdrawn
6	11564	Brigham Hall	0-6-0ST	1926
7	11565	Ponsonby Hall	,,	1927
8	11566	Hutton Hall	,,	1927
9	11567	Skiddaw Lodge	,,	*
10	11568	Millgrove	,,	1928

* Sold 1932 to Hartley Main Collieries, where it worked until 1956.

Caledonian Railway

The Caledonian was not a railway which ordinarily named its locomotives, but from time to time one or two of a new express class would be singled out for the distinction, the name being applied in hand painted lettering to a driving wheel splasher. Very few however were so treated, and all lost their names when they came into the L.M.S., in some cases earlier.

DRUMMOND 4-4-0's BUILT 1886/9

79   later   1079   Carbrook   124   later   1124   Eglinton

They were allotted L.M.S. Nos. 14297 and 14296 at the grouping, but only 14297 actually carried it and the engine was scrapped in 1928.

McINTOSH 4-4-0's 'DUNALASTAIR' CLASSES BUILT 1896/8

C.R. No.	L.M.S. No.	Name	Scrapped
721	14311	Dunalastair	1931
723	14313	Victoria	1933
724	14314	Jubilee	1930
766	14430	Dunalastair 2nd	1936
779	14335	Breadalbane	1939

McINTOSH EXPRESS 6' 6" 4-6-0's BUILT 1903/6

C.R. No.	L.M.S. No.	Name	Scrapped
50	14751	Sir James Thompson	1933
903	14752	Cardean	1930

'Cardean' can of course rank amongst the most famous locomotives of all time, and it was somewhat surprising that this engine at least was not allowed to retain its name after the amalgamation.

McINTOSH MIXED TRAFFIC 5' 9" 4-6-0's BUILT 1906

C.R. No.	L.M.S. No.	Name	Scrapped
909	14610	Sir James King	1933
911	14612	Barochan	1931

Glasgow and South Western Railway

Only one Glasgow and South Western engine acquired the dignity of a name, and this did not occur until 1922, within two years of the end of the Company's independent existence.

This 4-4-0 was a particularly interesting engine, in that when built by Mr J. Manson in 1897 it was, concurrently with Mr Webb's 4-4-0 on the L.N.W.R. and Mr Drummond's 4-2-2-0 No. 720 on the L.S.W.R., one of the first 4 cylinder engines to run in the British Isles.

As No. 11 and later 394 on the G. & S.W.R. it became L.M.S. No. 14509 at the grouping. It had been rebuilt in 1922 with a considerably larger boiler, and received the name 'Lord Glenarthur'. It was scrapped in 1934.

Highland Railway

Britain's most northerly railway, the Highland, named most of its express engines, and a number of its tanks also. It was somewhat addicted to renaming particularly in the case of the smaller engines, as it was at one time the practice to give an engine allocated to working a particular branch the name of the locality. If it was transferred elsewhere it had to be renamed accordingly.

The method of applying the names was by hand painting on the splashers or tank sides, and when William Stroudley went to the L.B. & S.C.R. in 1870 after his short term of office on the Highland he took the idea with him and applied it to his numerous engines that he built for the Brighton.

When the L.M.S. took over the Highland at the grouping they perpetuated the names except in the case of tank engines, although the hand painted type of lettering took on a somewhat different style. Even the few engines which lasted into B.R. days were allowed to retain their names to the end.

At the turn of the century the Highland possessed a most interesting collection of passenger locomotives of varying ages, ranging from somewhat ancient 2-4-0's, many of which had been rebuilt from 2-2-2's, several classes of 4-4-0's, and fifteen mixed traffic 4-6-0's introduced in 1894, the first of the type in the British Isles, but as these never bore names they do not come into this story. In the year 1900, however, there also appeared the first of the fine 'Castle' class 4-6-0's, which did much yeoman work on the difficult H.R. system until well after the grouping.

Dealing first with the 2-4-0's, these may be summarised as follows:—

1	Raigmore	46	Clachnacuddin/Kingussie
2	Aldourie	47	Lovat/Beauly/Bruce
3	Ballindalloch	48	Cadboll/Dingwall
28	Glenbarry/Grantown	49	Belladrum/Helmsdale
29	Highlander/Forres	50	Aultnaskiah/Badenoch
30	Prince	51	Caithness/Blair-Atholl
31	Princess	52	Dunphail
33	Atholl/Birnam	53	Stafford/Golspie
34	Seafield/Perthshire	54	Macduff
35	Kingsmills/Isla Bank	55	Cluny/Sutherland/Invergordon

Most of these disappeared fairly early in the century, some possibly even prior to 1900, but 'Isla Bank' lasted as No. 35A until about 1923.

STROUDLEY 0-6-0T's

During his short term of office on the Highland Mr Stroudley designed only one new class, of which three examples were built, two of them after his departure for the south. They were the forerunners of his much more numerous and better known 'Terriers' which he brought out on the Brighton.

56 Balnain/Dornoch   57 Lochgorm
16 later 49 St. Martins/Fort George

All lasted until the grouping, becoming L.M.S. Nos. 16118, 16119, and 16383. 'Lochgorm', then 57B, was still working at Inverness in 1928 in its Highland colours, albeit somewhat faded, but it went through the works once more in 1929 and emerged as L.M.S. 16119, losing its name. It lasted until 1932. The other two were scrapped in 1927.

'BRUCE' CLASS 4-4-0's

David Jones first main line engines for the H.R. was a class of fine 4-4-0's. The first ten came out in 1874:—

60	Bruce/Sutherland	65	Nairnshire/Dalraddy
61	The Duke/Duke	66	Ross-shire/Ardvuela
62	Perthshire/Huntingtower/	67	Cromartie
	Stemster/Aultwharrie		
63	Inverness-shire/Inverness	68	Caithness-shire/Caithness/
			Muirtown
64	Morayshire/Seafield	69	The Lord Provost/Sir James
			Aldourie

Others followed between 1876 and 1888, the later ones being slightly enlarged.

4 later 31   Ardross/Auchtertyre

71	Clachnacuddin	78	Lochalsh
72	Bruce/Grange	79	Atholl
73	Thurlow/Rosehaugh	80	Stafford
74	Beaufort	81	Colville
75	Breadalbane	82	Fife/Durn
76	Bruce	83	Cadboll/Monkland
77	Lovat	84	Dochfour

It will be noted that the name 'Bruce' turned up at various times on three different engines of the class.

No. 82 lasted into L.M.S. days as No. 14278, but it had already lost its name 'Durn' when the new large 4-4-0 No. 74 was built in 1916.

A larger version, known as the 'Straths' or 'Glens' appeared in 1892, twelve engines being built.

89	Sir George	95	Strathcarron
90	Tweeddale/Grandtully	96	Glentilt
91	Strathspey	97	Glenmore
92	Strathdearn/Glendean	98	Glentruim
93	Strathnairn	99	Glentromie
94	Strathtay	100	Glenbruar

Nos. 89, 92, 94, 95, 98 and 100 lasted into L.M.S. days, and became Nos. 14271–14276. They were scrapped between 1925 and 1930.

'NEEDLEFIELD'

There was in existence in 1900 a small 0-4-2T No. 1A named 'Needlefield' which had been rebuilt from a 0-4-0 Contractors engine built in 1863. It disappeared about 1904.

JONES 4-4-0T's

Three engines constructed by Mr Jones in 1879 for branch line work. They were originally built as 2-4-0T's.

17 later 50 Breadalbane/Aberfeldy
58 Burghead 59 Highlander

All survived the grouping to become L.M.S. Nos. 15012, 15010 and 15011, but without names, being scrapped between 1928 and 1932.

0-4-4T's

53 Strathpeffer/Lybster 25 Strathpeffer
40 Gordon Lennox

No. 53 was built by Mr Jones in 1890 and Nos. 25 and 40 (together with two others un-named) by Mr Drummond in 1905. They became L.M.S. Nos. 15050–15052, and No. 15051 survived Nationalisation to become B.R. No. 55051, being withdrawn in 1956. All however had lost their names at the grouping.

Before leaving the tank engines, mention must be made of two others built by the Duke of Sutherland for his own private use together with a saloon coach in which he travelled frequently over the Highland Railway.

The first was a 2-4-0T named 'Dunrobin' and it was replaced by a new 0-4-4T bearing the same name in 1892. The original engine then passed into the hands of the H.R., who numbered it 118, bearing the name 'Gordon Castle' and later 'Invergordon'. It lasted until 1922.

The second 'Dunrobin' never became Highland property, but remained in its shed at Golspie, for many years latterly unused, but was eventually acquired for preservation and for several years reposed at New Romney, in Kent, far removed from its original habitation. It has since travelled very much further—to Canada.

From 1896 onwards, commencing with the 'Loch' 4-4-0's, Mr David Jones' last engines, there was inaugurated a method of naming classes systematically with names of common origin embodying a series with the descriptive title 'Loch', 'Castle', and so on, common to all. This anticipated by several years what eventually became the later standard practice as carried out by the Great Western, although it had originally appeared on that line as long ago as 1837.

JONES' 'LOCH' CLASS 4-4-0's

119	Loch Insh	128	Loch Luichart
120	Loch Ness	129	Loch Maree
121	Loch Ericht	130	Loch Fannich
122	Loch Moy	131	Loch Shin
123	Loch-an-Dorb	132	Loch Naver
124	Loch Laggan	133	Loch Laoghal
125	Loch Tay	70	Loch Ashie
126	Loch Tummel	71	Loch Garve
127	Loch Garry	72	Loch Ruthven

The first fifteen engines were built in 1896, but the last three not until 1917, when the urgent necessity for new engines resulted in the construction of fresh examples of an old and well tried design rather than an unknown new one. These became L.M.S. Nos. 14379–14396, the last survivor being No. 14379, withdrawn in 1948.

SMALL 'BEN' CLASS 4-4-0

Mr Peter Drummond, who succeeded David Jones in 1896, commenced with a series of inside cylinder 4-4-0's (a radical departure from tradition on the Highland), of which twenty were built between 1898 and 1906.

1	Ben Nevis/ Ben-y-Gloe	7	Ben Attow	14	Ben Dearg
		8	Ben Clebrig	15	Ben Loyal
2	Ben Alder	9	Ben Rinnes	16	Ben Avon
3	Ben Wyvis	10	Ben Slioch	17	Ben Alligan
4	Ben More	11	Ben Macdhui	18	Ben Udlaman
5	Ben Vrackie	12	Ben Hope	19	Ben Bhach Ard
6	Ben Armin	13	Ben Alisky	20	Ben A'Bhuird

They became L.M.S. Nos. 14397–14416, and Nos. 2, 3 and 8 survived into Nationalisation days as B.R. 54398/9 and 54404. The last in service was 'Ben Alder', which was withdrawn in 1953 and retained for several years with a view to restoration although this did not materialise.

LARGE 'BEN' CLASS 4-4-0

An enlarged version of the previous class, six engines appearing in 1908 and 1909. Both classes bore names after mountains in the Highlands, but colloquially the later engines were referred to as the 'Big Bens' to distinguish them from their small sisters, the 'Wee Bens'.

61	Ben-na-Caillach at one time incorrectly spelt Ben-na-Caillich	68/65	Ben-a-Chait
63	Ben Mheadhoin	60	Ben Bhreac Mhor
66/64	Ben Mholach	62	Ben-a-Chaoruinn

They became L.M.S. Nos. 14417–14422 and were scrapped in the 1930's.

4-6-0 'CASTLE' CLASS

One of the earliest designs of 4-6-0 express passenger engines in the British Isles.

The first ten engines were built in 1900–2, followed by six more in 1910–13, and a final three (concurrently with the three 'Lochs' already referred to) in 1917.

140	Taymouth Castle	145	Murthly Castle
141	Ballindalloch Castle	146	Skibo Castle
142	Dunrobin Castle	147	Beaufort Castle
143	Gordon Castle	148	Cawdor Castle
144	Blair Castle	149	Duncraig Castle

30	Dunvegan Castle	43/29	Dalcross Castle
35	Urquhart Castle	50	Brodie Castle
26	Brahan Castle	58	Darnaway Castle
27	Thurso Castle	59	Foulis Castle
28	Cluny Castle		

These became L.M.S. Nos. 14675–14693. No. 14680 was scrapped in 1930 and the others between 1935 and 1947.

4-6-0 'RIVER' CLASS

Mr F. G. Smith's only engines during his short term of office. Six were built in 1915/16, but only two were actually delivered to the Highland as they were found to be too heavy for some of the bridges.

70 River Ness   71 River Spey

Together with the remaining four engines, they were disposed of almost immediately to the Caledonian Railway, on which they became Nos. 938–943 (without names).

As L.M.S. Nos. 14756–14761 they eventually found their way to the line for which they had been built. They were scrapped between 1939 and 1945.

CUMMING'S 4-4-0's

Mr C. Cumming succeeded Mr Smith and built two large 4-4-0's for the North Road in 1916.

73 Snaigow   74 Durn

They were not very good engines. They became L.M.S. Nos. 14522/3 and were scrapped in 1935/6.

'CLAN' CLASS 4-6-0's

Mr Cumming's 4-6-0's were a considerable improvement on his 4-4-0's. Four were built in 1919 and another four in 1921.

49	Clan Campbell	54	Clan Chattan
51	Clan Fraser	55	Clan Mackinnon
52	Clan Munro	56	Clan Mackenzie
53	Clan Stewart	57	Clan Cameron

They became Nos. 14762–14769. Two survived into Nationalisation, No. 14764, scrapped in 1948, and 14767, which became B.R. 54767 and which lasted until 1950.

London Midland and Scottish Railway

4-6-0 'PATRIOT' CLASS

The first two of these engines were rebuilds of L.N.W.R. 'Claughtons' and the next forty nominally so, although little if any of the original locomotive was incorporated. The last ten were definitely new constructions. Not all were named, but particulars of those which were are as follows:—

Original L.M.S. No.	Later L.M.S. No.	Name
5971	5500	Croxteth/Patriot
5902	5501	Sir Frank Ree/St. Dunstan's
5959	5502	Royal Naval Div.
5985	5503	The Leicestershire Regiment
5987	5504	Royal Signals
5949	5505	(Wemyss Bay)/ The Royal Army Ordnance Corps
5974	5506	The Royal Pioneer Corps
5936	5507	Royal Tank Corps
6005	5509	(Commando)/The Derbyshire Yeomanry
5942	5511	Isle of Man
5966	5512	Bunsen
5958	5513	(Sir W. A. Stanier)
5983	5514	Holyhead
5992	5515	Caernarvon
5982	5516	The Beds and Herts Regiment
6006	5518	Bradshaw
6008	5519	Lady Godiva
5954	5520	Llandudno
5933	5521	Rhyl
5973	5522	Prestatyn
6026	5523	Bangor
5907	5524	Blackpool
5916	5525	Colwyn Bay
5963	5526	Morecambe and Heysham
5944	5527	Southport
5996	5528	R.E.M.E.
5926	5529	Stephenson
6022	5530	Sir Frank Ree
6027	5531	Sir Frederick Harrison
6011	5532	Illustrious
5905	5533	Lord Rathmore
5935	5534	E. Tootal Broadhurst
5997	5535	Sir Herbert Walker, K.C.B.
6018	5536	Private W. Wood, V.C.
6015	5537	Private E. Sykes, V.C.
6000	5538	Giggleswick
5925	5539	E. C. Trench
5901	5540	Sir Robert Turnbull
5903	5541	Duke of Sutherland
	5542	(Dunoon)
	5543	Home Guard
	5545	Planet

Later L.M.S. No.	Name
5546	Fleetwood
5548	Lytham St. Anne's
5549	(R.A.M.C.)
5550	(Sir Henry Fowler)
5551	(Rothesay)

Names shown in brackets were allocated but never actually carried. No names were scheduled for the engines of the missing numbers in the above list. They became B.R. Nos. 45500–45551 and many were latterly rebuilt with taper boilers.

4-6-0's 'JUBILEE' CLASS

Stanier's intermediate express class 3 cylinder 4-6-0's, built 1934–6.

Number	Name	Number	Name
5552	Silver Jubilee	5584	North West Frontier
5553	Canada	5585	Hyderabad
5554	Ontario	5586	Mysore
5555	Quebec	5587	Baroda
5556	Nova Scotia	5588	Kashmir
5557	New Brunswick	5589	Gwalior
5558	Manitoba	5590	Travancore
5559	British Columbia	5591	Udaipur
5560	Prince Edward Island	5592	Indore
5561	Saskatchewan	× 5593	Kolhapur
5562	Alberta	5594	Bhopal
5563	Australia	5595	Southern Rhodesia
5564	New South Wales	× 5596	Bahamas
5565	Victoria	5597	Barbados
5566	Queensland	5598	Basutoland
5567	South Australia	5599	Bechuanaland
5568	Western Australia	5600	Bermuda
5569	Tasmania	5601	British Guiana
5570	New Zealand	5602	British Honduras
5571	South Africa	5603	Solomon Islands
5572	Irish Free State/Eire	5604	Ceylon
5573	Newfoundland	5605	Cyprus
5574	India	5606	Falkland Islands
5575	Madras	5607	Fiji
5576	Bombay	5608	Gibraltar
5577	Bengal	5609	Gilbert and Ellice Islands
5578	United Provinces	5610	Gold Coast/Ghana
5579	Punjab	5611	Hong Kong
5580	Burma	5612	Jamaica
5581	Bihar and Orissa	5613	Kenya
5582	Central Provinces	5614	Leeward Islands
5583	Assam	5615	Malay States

Number	Name
5616	Malta/Malta G.C.
5617	Mauritius
5618	New Hebrides
5619	Nigeria
5620	North Borneo
5621	Northern Rhodesia
5622	Nyasaland
5623	Palestine
5624	St. Helena
5625	Sarawak
5626	Seychelles
5627	Sierra Leone
5628	Somaliland
5629	Straits Settlements
5630	Swaziland
5631	Tanganyika
5632	Tonga
5633	Trans-Jordan/Aden
5634	Trinidad
5635	Tobago
5636	Uganda
5637	Windward Islands
5638	Zanzibar
5639	Raleigh
5640	Frobisher
5641	Sandwich
5642	Boscawen
5643	Rodney
5644	Howe
5645	Collingwood
5646	Napier
5647	Sturdee
5648	Wemyss
5649	Hawkins
5650	Blake
5651	Shovell
5652	Hawke
5653	Barham
5654	Hood
5655	Keith
5656	Cochrane
5657	Tyrwhitt
5658	Keyes
5659	Drake
5660	Rooke
5661	Vernon

Number	Name
5662	Kempenfelt
5663	Jervis
5664	Nelson
5665	Lord Rutherford of Nelson
5666	Cornwallis
5667	Jellicoe
5668	Madden
5669	Fisher
5670	Howard of Effingham
5671	Prince Rupert
5672	Anson
5673	Keppel
5674	Duncan
5675	Hardy
5676	Codrington
5677	Beatty
5678	De Robeck
5679	Armada
5680	Camperdown
5681	Aboukir
5682	Trafalgar
5683	Hogue
5684	Jutland
5685	Barfleur
5686	St. Vincent
5687	Neptune
5688	Polyphemus
5689	Ajax
5690	Leander
5691	Orion
5692	Cyclops
5693	Agamemnon
5694	Bellerophon
5695	Minotaur
5696	Arethusa
5697	Achilles
5698	Mars
5699	Galatea
5700	Britannia/Amethyst
5701	Conqueror
5702	Colossus
5703	Thunderer
5704	Leviathan
5705	Seahorse
5706	Express
5707	Valiant

Number	Name	Number	Name
5708	Resolution	5726	Vindictive
5709	Implacable	5727	Inflexible
5710	Irresistible	5728	Defiance
5711	Courageous	5729	Furious
5712	Victory	5730	Ocean
5713	Renown	5731	Perseverance
5714	Revenge	5732	Sanspareil
5715	Invincible	5733	Novelty
5716	Swiftsure	5734	Meteor
5717	Dauntless	5735	Comet
5718	Dreadnought	5736	Phoenix
5719	Glorious	5737	Atlas
5720	Indomitable	5738	Samson
5721	Impregnable	5739	Ulster
5722	Defence	5740	Munster
5723	Fearless	5741	Leinster
5724	Warspite	5742	Connaught
5725	Repulse		

All became B.R. Nos. 45552–45742. No. 45637 was scrapped in 1952 after the Harrow accident, but withdrawal on a general scale did not commence until 1960/1.

L.M.S. Class 5's—

STANIER MIXED TRAFFIC CLASS 5 4-6-0's

This well known and numerous class eventually totalled no less than 842 engines, but only four of them were named:—

Number	Name	Number	Name
5154	The Lanarkshire Yeomanry	5157	The Glasgow Highlander
5156	The Ayrshire Yeomanry	5158	The Glasgow Yeomanry

They became 45154 etc. on Nationalisation.

4-6-0 'ROYAL SCOT' CLASS

Sir Henry Fowler's main line express engine for the L.M.S., built 1927–1930. The first 25 were turned out with regimental names, but Nos. 6125–6149 were at first named after old time locomotives, and were provided also with exceedingly attractive brass plaques bearing etched outlines of the engines in question. It was most unfortunate that a later decision to name all of them after regiments resulted in the removal of these picturesque plaques.

Number	Name	Number	Name
6100	Royal Scot*	6103	Royal Scots Fusilier
6101	Royal Scots Grey	6104	Scottish Borderer
6102	Black Watch	6105	Cameron Highlander

*The additional nameplate for some time carried on the smokebox door was titled " THE ROYAL SCOT ".

Number	Name	Number	Name
6106	Gordon Highlander	6140	Hector/The King's Royal Rifle Corps
6107	Argyll and Sutherland Highlander	6141	Caledonian/The North Staffordshire Regt.
6108	Seaforth Highlander	6142	Lion/The York and Lancaster Regt.
6109	Royal Engineer		
6110	Grenadier Guardsman	6143	Mail/The South Staffordshire Regt.
6111	Royal Fusilier		
6112	Sherwood Forester	6144	Ostrich/The Hon. Artillery Company
6113	Cameronian		
6114	Coldstream Guardsman	6145	Condor/The Duke of Wellington's Regt. (West Riding)
6115	Scots Guardsman		
6116	Irish Guardsman		
6117	Welsh Guardsman	6146	Jenny Lind/The Rifle Brigade
6118	Royal Welch Fusilier		
6119	Lancashire Fusilier	6147	Courier/The Northamptonshire Regt.
6120	Royal Inniskilling Fusilier		
6121	H.L.I./ Highland Light Infantry, City of Glasgow Regiment	6148	Velocipede/The Manchester Regt.
		6149	Lady of the Lake/The Middlesex Regt.
6122	Royal Ulster Rifleman	6150	The Life Guardsman
6123	Royal Irish Fusilier	6151	The Royal Horse Guardsman
6124	London Scottish		
6125	Lancashire Witch/3rd Carabinier	6152	The King's Dragoon Guardsman
6126	Sanspareil/Royal Army Service Corps	6153	The Royal Dragoon
6127	Novelty/Old Contemptibles	6154	The Hussar
6128	Meteor/The Lovat Scouts	6155	The Lancer
6129	Comet/The Scottish Horse	6156	The South Wales Borderer
6130	Liverpool/The West Yorkshire Regt.	6157	The Royal Artilleryman
		6158	The Loyal Regt.
6131	Planet/The Royal Warwickshire Regiment	6159	The Royal Air Force
		6160	Queen Victoria's Rifleman
6132	Phoenix/The King's Regt.	6161	King's Own
6133	Vulcan/The Green Howards	6162	Queen's Westminster Rifleman
6134	Atlas/The Cheshire Regt.		
6135	Samson/The East Lancashire Regt.	6163	Civil Service Rifleman
		6164	The Artist's Rifleman
6136	Goliath/The Border Regt.	6165	The Ranger (12th London Regt.)
6137	Vesta/The Prince of Wales Volunteers(South Lancs)		
		6166	London Rifle Brigade
6138	Fury/The London Irish Rifleman	6167	The Hertfordshire Regt.
		6168	The Girl Guide
6139	Ajax/The Welch Regt.	6169	The Boy Scout

t North of Scotland type of nameplate as seen on the restored 'Gordon Highlander'.

Great North of Scotland Railway—The painted name of 'Gordon Highlander' before restoration.

of the N.B.R. 0-6-0's which served overseas g the first world war and was given a commemoration name on return.

Original North British style of lettering as can be seen on the restored 'Glen Douglas'.

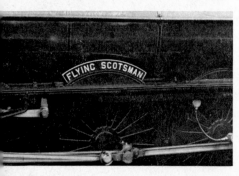

Two modified forms of lettering as applied by the L.N.E.R. to North British engines.

Nameplate of Gresley Pacific No. 4472.

Nameplate of Gresley 2-6-2 No. 60964.

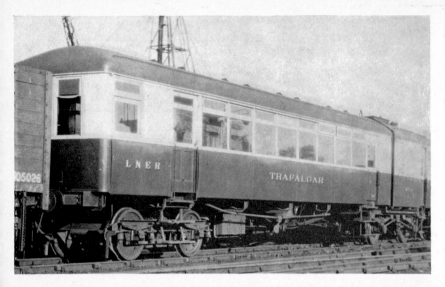

'Trafalgar'
showing the style
in which the
L.N.E.R. Sentinel railcars were
named.

[E. R. Wethersett

The ornamental fox formerly carried by the streamliner No. 2512 when built in 1935.

'Hunt' class locomotive 'The Percy' showing the fox with which these plates were surmounted.

Gresley 3-cylinder K4 2-6-0 No. 3444 (eventually B.R. 61996).

G.N.R. 2-6-0 No. 61783 after transfer to the Scottish Region. The dummy splasher to accommodate the nameplate will be noted.

L.B. & S.C.R. Stroudley 0-4-2T No. 233, showing the standard type of painting adopted in his day.

L.B. & S.C.R. 'Gladstone' type 0-4-2, one of the engines which retained its name during the Marsh regime.

L.B. & S.C.R. 'Atlantic' No. 39 'La France', named in honour of a visit by the French President to this country.

...ame and Commemoration plates ... the L.B. & S.C.R. War Memorial engine, 4-6-4T No. 333.

The only S.E. & C.R. engine which actually carried a nameplate during the lifetime of that Company as such. It was a former London, Chatham and Dover locomotive, whose few other named engines lost their plates on amalgamation, but this one was apparently overlooked for a time.

[*H. D. Hewitt*

S.E. & C.R. Maunsell 4-4-0 No. 763, named temporarily by volunteers during the 1926 strike, and which it carried for several months afterwards.

One of the ill-fated 'River' class tanks of the S.R., later converted to tender engines and de-named.

In 1933 No. 6152 exchanged name and number with 6100 and visited the United States. The later No. 46152 is therefore the original 'Royal Scot'. Withdrawal of this class commenced in 1962. All were withdrawn by 1965, but Nos. 6100 and 6115 have been preserved privately.

FOWLER HIGH PRESSURE 4-6-0

Built in 1930, this experimental engine was constructed on the lines of the 'Royal Scots' but was a compound with super high pressure boiler. It was not a success, and was eventually rebuilt as a 3 cylinder simple with taper boiler, to which form all the 'Royal Scots' were eventually reconstructed.

As a compound it was No. 6399 'Fury' and the etched plaque of the outline of the old engine of that name was transferred from No. 6138. On rebuild it became No. 6170 'British Legion'. As B.R. No. 46170 it was scrapped in 1962.

STANIER 'PRINCESS' PACIFICS

Stanier's first series of Pacifics built in 1933/5, consisted of twelve engines, Nos. 6200/1, 6203–12.

Number	Name	Number	Name
6200	The Princess Royal	6207	Princess Arthur of
6201	Princess Elizabeth		Connaught
6203	Princess Margaret Rose	6208	Princess Helena Victoria
6204	Princess Louise	6209	Princess Beatrice
6205	Princess Victoria	6210	Lady Patricia
6206	Princess Marie Louise	6211	Queen Maud
		6212	Duchess of Kent

All were taken out of service in 1961 and 1962, but Nos. 6201 and 6203 have been preserved privately.

4-6-0 'TURBOMOTIVE' No. 6202

This engine, built in 1933 as an experimental turbine engine, ran in this form until 1952 and was not named. In that year it was reconstructed as an ordinary reciprocating engine, and was named 'Princess Anne', No. 46202. Its life in this condition was exceedingly short, however, as it was involved in the disastrous Harrow accident of that year, and damaged beyond repair.

STANIER'S 'CORONATION' AND 'DUCHESS' PACIFICS

Sir William Stanier's later Pacifics were built between 1937 and 1948. Most of them were originally built with streamlined casing, but this has since been removed. The nameplates on this class are of rectangular shape on the side of the boiler barrel, as distinct from the semi circular type over the splasher as in earlier L.M.S. classes:—

Number	Name	Number	Name
6220	Coronation	6240	City of Coventry
6221	Queen Elizabeth	6241	City of Edinburgh
6222	Queen Mary	6242	City of Glasgow
6223	Princess Alice	6243	City of Lancaster
6224	Princess Alexandra	6244	City of Leeds/King George VI
6225	Duchess of Gloucester		
6226	Duchess of Norfolk	6245	City of London
6227	Duchess of Devonshire	6246	City of Manchester
6228	Duchess of Rutland	6247	City of Liverpool
✕ 6229	Duchess of Hamilton	6248	City of Leeds
6230	Duchess of Buccleuch	6249	City of Sheffield
6231	Duchess of Atholl	6250	City of Lichfield
6232	Duchess of Montrose	6251	City of Nottingham
✕ 6233	Duchess of Sutherland	6252	City of Leicester
6234	Duchess of Abercorn	6253	City of St. Albans
✕ 6235	City of Birmingham	6254	City of Stoke-on-Trent
6236	City of Bradford	6255	City of Hereford
6237	City of Bristol	6256	Sir William A. Stanier, F.R.S.
6238	City of Carlisle		
6239	City of Chester	46257	City of Sheffield

No 46257 appeared in 1948, and never ran as an L.M.S. engine. All of the class, of course, became 46220–46257. No. 6229 went to the U.S.A. in 1939 temporarily exchanging numbers with No. 6220, which were put back on return. The present No. 46220 is in consequence not the actual engine which visited the United States. All withdrawn by 1965, but Nos. 6229, 6233 and 6235 have been preserved privately.

FOWLER 2-6-4T's

One of these engines, No. 2313, was temporarily named 'The Prince' in hand painted lettering on the tank sides following a visit by the Duke of Windsor in 1928 when the engine was under construction. It was removed on the engine's first repaint.

III
The
London North Eastern Group

Great Northern Railway

Like its rival, the Midland, the G.N.R. never pursued a policy of naming its locomotives, and likewise bestowed this distinction on only two of its locomotives whilst it retained its individual identity.

In 1898 Mr H. A. Ivatt built at Doncaster the first 4-4-2, or 'Atlantic', engine to run in these islands. It was the forerunner of the famous series of locomotives of this type which made history on the G.N.R. Numbered 990, it was at first unnamed, but later received the appellation 'Henry Oakley', carried on two small brass plates on each pair of splashers. It became L.N.E.R. No. 3990 at the grouping, and was withdrawn in 1937. It is now preserved in York Museum.

In 1922, when the grouping of the railways was imminent, Sir Nigel Gresley brought out the first of his famous Pacifics, and in commemoration of the shortly expected demise of the Great Northern Railway, he appropriately named the first of them, No. 1470, 'Great Northern'. The second engine of the class to appear before the amalgamation, No. 1471, was turned out unnamed, and although it later under L.N.E.R. auspices received the name 'Sir Frederick Banbury', it cannot be strictly regarded as an engine named by the Great Northern Railway Company. No. 1472, probably the most famous of them all, did not appear until 1923, and must therefore be classified as an L.N.E.R. engine.

No. 1470 became L.N.E.R. 4470 and under the 1946 renumbering scheme, No. 113 (it was at first intended to be No. 500, but never bore this number). It had already been completely rebuilt in 1945 in the form in which it became the prototype of Mr Thompson's A1 class. It later became, and is still running at the time of writing (1963) B.R. No. 60113.

No. 1471 likewise became L.N.E.R. 4471, then 102, and eventually B.R. 60102, and was withdrawn in 1961.

This, however, is not quite the whole story as regards the naming of Great Northern engines proper, as a few years after the grouping a number of Mr Gresley's K2 class 2-6-0 engines, which had been built between 1918 and 1921, were transferred to Scotland. Several of these were allocated for working over the West Highland line, a duty they performed for many years.

They were named after Scottish lochs, the individual engines being as follows:—

First L.N.E.R. No.	Renumbered 1946	Name
4674	1764	Loch Arkaig
4682	1772	Loch Lochy
4684	1774	Loch Garry
4685	1775	Loch Treig
4691	1781	Loch Morar
4692	1782	Loch Eil
4693	1783	Loch Shiel
4697	1787	Loch Quoich
4698	1788	Loch Rannoch
4699	1789	Loch Laidon
4700	1790	Loch Lomond
4701	1791	Loch Laggan
4704	1794	Loch Oich

Their original G.N.R. numbers were 1674, 1682, etc., and all came into B.R. stock in 1948, with the addition of 60000 to their later numbers, 61764, 61772, etc. Some of them lasted until 1961.

North Eastern Railway

Of the four largest railways at the time of the 1923 grouping, two (the L.N.W.R. and G.W.R.) had consistently followed a policy of naming all of their principal passenger engines, whilst the remaining two (the Midland and the North Eastern) had pursued a directly opposite principle, with but one or two odd deviations from this policy.

The exception in the case of the North Eastern was an engine with an interesting history. Some authorities regard this engine as dating back to the year 1851, but although there was an engine constructed in that year bearing the same name, it can really only be regarded as an ancestor of a later machine built in 1869, which was in fact an entirely new locomotive. It was built by E. Fletcher as a 2-2-2 well tank. It was numbered 66, and later lost its name, 'Aerolite' although this was later to be restored in 1902. After sundry rebuildings it eventually became the 2-2-4T which was better known in more recent years, and is now preserved in York Museum, having been last active in service in 1933.

In 1922, when the amalgamation of the pre-grouping companies was imminent, Sir Vincent Raven had in hand a design of Pacifics for the N.E.R., and five of them were turned out during that year. Although perhaps moderately capable engines, they had little chance of competing with Gresley's much more successful G.N.R. machines, and were destined for a short life, all being withdrawn in 1936 and 1937. Their names and numbers were as follows:—

2400 City of Newcastle
2401 City of Kingston-upon-Hull
2402 City of York
2403 City of Durham
2404 City of Ripon

Great Central Railway

The G.C.R. grew from the Manchester, Sheffield and Lincolnshire Railway when that concern extended its line to London in 1900. The M.S. & L.R. was one of the railways which had not followed the practice of naming its engines, and this policy was more or less followed by Mr Robinson for several years subsequently, although one or two odd engines were given names prior to 1913, after which the practice increased to some extent with the coming of the well-known 'Directors'.

ROBINSON 4-4-0's BUILT 1901–1904 (L.N.E.R. CLASS D9)

The class consisted of forty engines, but only the following received names

G.C.R. No.	1st L.N.E.R. No.	1946 L.N.E.R. No.	B.R. No.	Name
104	5104	(2326)	—	Queen Alexandra
110	5110	—	—	King George V
1014	6014	2301	—	Sir Alexander*
1021	6021	2307	62307	Queen Mary

* Name removed about 1913

All scrapped by 1950.

ROBINSON 3 CYLINDER COMPOUND 4-4-2's BUILT 1905-6 (L.N.E.R. CLASS C5)

G.C.R. No.	1st L.N.E.R. No.	1946 L.N.E.R. No.	B.R. No.	Name
258	5258	2895	—	The Right Hon. Viscount Cross, G.C.B., G.C.S.I.
259	5259	2896	—	King Edward VII
364	5364	2897	—	Lady Henderson/Lady Faringdon
365	5365	2898	—	Sir William Pollitt

All scrapped 1947.

ROBINSON 6' 9" 4-4-0's (L.N.E.R. CLASS D10)

G.C.R. No.	L.N.E.R. No.	1946 L.N.E.R. No.	Name
429	5429	2650	Sir Alexander Henderson/ Sir Douglas Haig/Prince Henry
430	5430	2651	Purdon Viccars
431	5431	2652	Edwin A. Beazley

G.C.R. No.	L.N.E.R. No.	1946 L.N.E.R. No.	Name
432	5432	2653	Sir Edward Fraser
433	5433	2654	Walter Burgh Gair
434	5434	2655	The Earl of Kerry
435	5435	2656	Sir Clement Royds
436	5436	2657	Sir Berkeley Sheffield
437	5437	2658	Charles Stuart-Wortley/ Prince George
438	5438	2659	Worsley-Taylor

All became B.R. 62650–62659 and were scrapped between 1953 and 1955.

ROBINSON 6′ 9″ 4-4-0's (L.N.E.R. CLASS D11)

G.C.R. No.	L.N.E.R. No.	1946 L.N.E.R. No.	Name
501	5501	2665	Mons
502	5502	2666	Zeebrugge
503	5503	2667	Somme
504	5504	2668	Jutland
505	5505	2669	Ypres
506	5506	2660	Butler-Henderson
507	5507	2661	Gerard Powys Dewhurst
508	5508	2662	Prince of Wales
509	5509	2663	Prince Albert
510	5510	2664	Princess Mary
511	5511	2670	Marne

All became B.R. 62660–62670 and were scrapped in 1959/60 with the exception of No. 506, which has been restored to its original condition and preserved.

ROBINSON 6′ 7″ 4-6-0's (L.N.E.R. CLASS B4)

Class of 10 engines built 1906, but only one was named.

G.C.R. No.	L.N.E.R. No.	1946 L.N.E.R. No.	Name
1097	6097	1482	Immingham

Scrapped 1950.

ROBINSON 5' 7" 4-6-0's (L.N.E.R. CLASS B8)

G.C.R. No.	L.N.E.R. No.	1946 L.N.E.R. No.	Name
4	5004	1349	Glenalmond
279	5279	1358	Earl Kitchener of Khartoum
439	5439	1350	Sutton Nelthorpe
446	5446	1357	Earl Roberts of Kandahar

Scrapped 1947–1949.

ROBINSON 6' 9" 4-6-0's (L.N.E.R. CLASS B2)

G.C.R. No.	L.N.E.R. No.	1946 L.N.E.R. No.	Name
423	5423	1490	Sir Sam Fay
424	5424	—	City of Lincoln
425	5425	1491	City of Manchester
426	5426	—	City of Chester
427	5427	1492	City of London*
428	5428	1493	City of Liverpool

* Name removed 1937

All scrapped 1944–1947.

ROBINSON 6' 9" 4-CYLINDER 4-6-0's (L.N.E.R. CLASS B3)

G.C.R. No.	L.N.E.R. No.	1946 L.N.E.R. No.	Name
1164	6164	1495	Earl Beatty
1165	6165	1496	Valour*
1166	6166	1497	Earl Haig†
1167	6167	1498	Lloyd George‡
1168	6168	1499	Lord Stuart of Wortley
1169	6169	1494	Lord Faringdon

All scrapped 1947–1949.

* The G.C.R. War Memorial engine. The plate also bore the wording 'In memory of G.C.R. employees who lost their lives during the Great War 1914–1918'.

† Name removed, 1943   ‡ Name removed, 1923

Great Eastern Railway

It is a curious fact that, of the major pre-grouping railway companies, three of them (the other two being the Midland and the Great Northern, see pages 65 and 83) managed to name the exact total of two engines out of the several thousand they owned during their existence.

The first G.E.R. engine to bear a name was one of Holden's 2-4-0 express engines, class T19, No. 760, which was built at Stratford in 1890. In 1893 it was adapted for oil burning, with which the G.E.R. were conducting considerable experiments at the time, and appropriately named 'Petrolea'. Although many of this class were later rebuilt with large boiler and in many cases as 4-4-0's, lasting in a number of cases to the late 1930's, No. 760 was never so treated and went during the earlier part of the century.

In 1900, Mr James Holden brought out the first of his famous 4-4-0's which were destined to become the mainstay of express work on the G.E.R. main lines for many years to come. Numbered after the year of its birth, No. 1900 was christened 'Claud Hamilton', and thereafter the class was always affectionately known as 'Clauds'. They underwent many modifications and rebuildings in the course of their history, and after an honourable career the last of them did not finally disappear until 1960. Handsome engines they were, too, in their original state, and it is the greatest pity that one of them has not been preserved.

'Claud Hamilton' itself underwent complete rebuilding by Mr Gresley in 1933, when the brass nameplate, carried on the splasher, was replaced by a new style cast plate. In 1942 the engine was temporarily renumbered 7770, and in 1946 again altered to 2500. It was withdrawn from service in 1947, and the nameplates were transferred to another engine of the class, No. 2546 (originally 1855), which in turn became B.R. No. 62546 and was scrapped in 1957.

Colne Valley and Halstead Railway

	Haverhill	0-6-0T	Built	1873
2	Halstead	2-4-2T	„	1887
3	Colne	„	„	1887
4	Hedingham	„	„	1894

'Haverhill' was sold to the South Hetton Colliery, where it remained until scrapped in 1948. Nos. 2 and 3 became L.N.E.R. 8312 and 8313 at the grouping, lasting until 1930 and 1927 respectively. No. 4 was scrapped in 1923 without being renumbered.

North British Railway

Naming on the N.B.R. was fairly common in Drummond's day until 1882, in which year Matthew Holmes took charge, after which it suffered an eclipse until the present century, when W. P. Reid assumed the position of C.M.E. This gentleman reintroduced the practice with the appearance of his 'Atlantics' in 1906, followed by the 'Scott' class 4-4-0 and finally his 'Glens'.

'SCOTT' CLASS 4-4-0's 6' 6" DRIVING WHEELS, BUILT 1909–1920. (L.N.E.R. CLASS D29 and D30)

Original N.B.R. No.	*2nd L.N.E.R. No. (1946)*	*Name*
243	2406	Meg Merrilees
244	2407	Madge Wildfire
245	2408	Bailie Nicol Jarvie
338	2409	Helen MacGregor
339	2410	Ivanhoe
340	2411	Lady of Avenel
359	2412	Dirk Hatteraick
360	2413	Guy Mannering
361	(2414)	Vich Ian Vohr
362	2415	Ravenswood
363	2417	Hal o' the Wynd
400	(2416)	The Dougal Cratur
409	2418	The Pirate
410	2419	Meg Dods
411	2420	Dominie Sampson
412	2421	Laird o' Monkbarns
413	2422	Caleb Balderstone
414	2423	Dugald Dalgetty
415	2424	Claverhouse
416	2425	Ellangowan
417	2426	Cuddie Headrigg
418	2427	Dumbiedykes
419	2428	Talisman
420	2429	The Abbot
421	2430	Jingling Geordie
422	2431	Kenilworth
423	2432	Quentin Durward
424	2433	Lady Rowena
425	2434	Kettledrummle
426	2435	Norna
427	2436	Lord Glenvarloch
428	2437	Adam Woodcock
497	2438	Peter Poundtext
498	2439	Father Ambrose
499	2440	Wandering Willie
500	2441	Black Duncan
501	2442	Simon Glover
895	2400	Rob Roy
896	2401	Dandie Dinmont
897	2402	Redgauntlet
898	2403	Sir Walter Scott
899	2404	Jeanie Deans
900	2405	The Fair Maid

At the grouping the original N.B.R. numbers were increased by 9000, thus becoming 9243, etc., until the complete renumbering took place in 1946 when the class became 2400–2442. These numbers were increased by 60000 on Nationalisation, but a few were scrapped without actually being renumbered. The class became extinct in 1959.

'GLEN' CLASS 4-4-0's 6' 0" WHEELS, BUILT 1913–1920.

A smaller wheeled version of the 'Scotts' for intermediate passenger service, and in particular for work on the West Highland line. L.N.E.R. class D34.

Original N.B.R. No.	2nd L.N.E.R. No. (1946)	Name
34	2492	Glen Garvin
35	2493	Glen Gloy
100	2477	Glen Dochart
149	2467	Glenfinnan
153	2480	Glen Fruin
221	2468	Glen Orchy
241	2481	Glen Ogle
242	2482	Glen Mamie
256	2469	Glen Douglas
258	2470	Glen Roy
266	2471	Glen Falloch
270	2483	Glen Garry
278	2484	Glen Lyon
281	2485	Glen Murran
287	2486	Glen Gyle
291	2478	Glen Quoich
298	2479	Glen Shiel
307	2472	Glen Nevis
405	2473	Glen Spean
406	2474	Glen Croe
407	2475	Glen Beasdale
408	2476	Glen Sloy
490	2489	Glen Dessary
492	2494	Glen Gour
493	2495	Glen Luss
494	2496	Glen Loy
495	2497	Glen Mallie
496	2498	Glen Moidart
502	2490	Glen Fintaig
503	2487	Glen Arklet
504	2488	Glen Aladale
505	2491	Glen Cona

The first L.N.E.R. and the B.R. renumberings followed the same pattern as the 'Scotts'. The engines were taken out of service between 1946 and 1961, but No. 256 'Glen Douglas' was preserved in working order and restored to the old N.B.R. colours. It is now housed in Glasgow Museum.

'ATLANTICS' BUILT 1906–1921. (L.N.E.R. CLASSES C10 AND C11)

509	9509	Duke of Rothesay
510	9510	The Lord Provost
868	9868	Aberdonian
869	9869	Dundonian/Bonnie Dundee
870	9870	Bon Accord
871	9871	Thane of Fife
872	9872	Auld Reekie
873	9873	Saint Mungo
874	9874	Dunedin
875	9875	Midlothian
876	9876	Waverley
877	9877	Liddesdale
878	9878	Hazeldean
879	9879	Abbotsford
880	9880	Tweeddale
881	9881	Borderer
901	9901	St. Johnstoun
902	9902	Highland Chief
903	9903	Cock o' the North/ Aberdonian
904	9904	Holyrood
905	9905	Buccleuch
906	9906	Teribus

At the grouping they became L.N.E.R. 9509 etc., but as they all disappeared between 1933 and 1939 they were never included in the 1946 renumbering.

HOLMES 0-6-0's (L.N.E.R. CLASS J36)

This numerous class dates from the period 1888–1900. During the first world war 25 of them were sent overseas, mainly if not entirely to France. On their return they were given suitable commemorative names, which they carried in most cases for the rest of their existence. In a few cases they lost their names at one repaint, but had them restored on a subsequent visit to shops. They are somewhat remarkable in that the naming of freight engines on the main line companies has always been exceedingly rare. It will be noted that some of the names were duplicated by G.C.R. Directors class engines, which also of course came into L.N.E.R. stock in 1923, but owing to difference of location it is doubtful whether they ever came into contact with one another, and it is extremely unlikely that any confusion could have arisen.

Original N.B.R. No.	2nd L.N.E.R. No. (1946)	Name
176	5217	French
605		St. Quentin
608		Foch
611	5268	Allenby
612	5269	Ypres
615		Verdun
620		Rawlinson
621		Munro
627		Petain
628	5216	Byng
631		Aisne
643	5219	Arras
646	5222	Somme
647	5223	Albert
648	5224	Mons
650	5226	Haig
657	5233	Plumer
659	5235	Gough
660	5236	Horne
661		Ole Bill
662		Birdwood
666		Marne
673	5243	Maude
676		Rheims
682	5253	Joffre

All survived to have 9000 added to their numbers at the grouping, but a number of them were scrapped in the later 1920's and the 1930's and consequently were not included in the 1946 renumbering scheme. Most of those that did also came into B.R. hands and had their numbers increased by 60000. About eight of these were still in existence in 1962. 'Maude' is being preserved.

Great North of Scotland Railway

It was not until the last phase of its existence that the G.N. o S.R. gave any thought to naming its locomotives. The final batch of a long series of 4-4-0's of various classes, however, which were built in 1920, were as follows:-

Original G. N. o S. No.	2nd L.N.E.R. No. (1946)	Name
45	2273	George Davidson
46	2274	Benachie
47	2275	Sir David Stewart
48	2276	Andrew Bain
49	2277	Gordon Highlander
50	2278	Hatton Castle
52	2279	Glen Grant
54	2280	Southesk

The names were on cast iron plates around the rim of the leading splasher, although latterly the plates were removed and the names painted on.

The numbers after the grouping were increased by 6800, becoming 6845, etc. The last in traffic was 'Gordon Highlander' and in 1958 it was restored in working order to its G. N.o S.R. livery (with nameplate replaced). It is now housed in Glasgow Museum.

London and North Eastern Railway

The L.N.E.R. at its formation in 1923 possessed few named locomotives. Of its constituents, only two, the Great Central and the North British, had named some of their later passenger locomotives, and even these were not greatly numerous.

Very soon after the amalgamation, however, the naming of the principal passenger classes was undertaken systematically and as a matter of course.

Under construction at the time of the grouping were the first of Sir Nigel Gresley's world famous Pacifics. The first two, Nos. 1470 and 1471, had come out in 1922 as Great Northern engines, and have been dealt with under that heading. Thereafter followed a further ten, turned out as L.N.E.R. 1472N to 1481N and at first without names. Eventually the whole series built between 1923 and 1925 ran as follows:—

1st L.N.E.R. No.	*3rd L.N.E.R. No.* (*1946*)	*Name*
4472	103	Flying Scotsman
4473	104	Solario
4474	105	Victor Wild
4475	106	Flying Fox
4476	107	Royal Lancer
4477	108	Gay Crusader
4478	109	Hermit
4479	110	Robert the Devil
4480	111	Enterprise
4481	112	St. Simon
2500	35	Windsor Lad
2501	36	Colombo
2502	37	Hyperion
2503	38	Firdaussi
2504	39	Sandwich
2505	40	Cameronian
2506	41	Salmon Trout
2507	42	Singapore
2508	43	Brown Jack
2543	44	Melton
2544	45	Lemberg
2545	46	Diamond Jubilee
2546	47	Donovan

1st L.N.E.R. No.	3rd L.N.E.R. No. (1946)	Name
2547	48	Doncaster
2548	49	Galtee More
2549	50	Persimmon
2550	51	Blink Bonny
2551	52	Prince Palatine
2552	53	Sansovino
2553	54	Manna/Prince of Wales
2554	55	Woolwinder
2555	56	Centenary
2556	57	Ormonde
2557	58	Blair Athol
2558	59	Tracery
2559	60	The Tetrarch
2560	61	Pretty Polly
2561	62	Minoru
2562	63	Isinglass
2563	64	William Whitelaw/Tagalie
2564	65	Knight of Thistle
2565	66	Merry Hampton
2566	67	Ladas
2567	68	Sir Visto
2568	69	Sceptre
2569	70	Gladiateur
2570	71	Tranquil
2571	72	Sunstar
2572	73	St. Gatien
2573	74	Harvester
2574	75	St. Frusquin
2575	76	Galopin
2576	77	The White Knight
2577	78	Night Hawk
2578	79	Bayardo
2579	80	Dick Turpin
2580	81	Shotover
2581	82	Neil Gow
2582	83	Sir Hugo
2595	84	Trigo
2596	85	Manna
2597	86	Gainsborough
2598	87	Blenheim
2599	88	Book Law
2743	89	Felstead
2744	90	Grand Parade
2745	91	Captain Cuttle
2746	92	Fairway
2747	93	Coronach

1st L.N.E.R. No.	3rd L.N.E.R. No. (1946)	Name
2748	94	Colorado
2749	95	Flamingo
2750	96	Papyrus
2751	97	Humorist
2752	98	Spion Kop
2795	99	Call Boy
2796	100	Spearmint
2797	101	Cicero

It will be noted that the second column refers to the third L.N.E.R. numbering. This is owing to the fact that in 1944 an initial scheme was drawn up under which these engines were to have been numbered in the 500's, and a few actually appeared thus. It was however very soon modified in favour of the 35–112 series. Under Nationalisation all became 60035–60112. Withdrawals commenced in 1959. No. 4472 has been preserved in working order under private auspices and frequently appears on enthusiasts' specials.

GRESLEY A4 STREAMLINED 'PACIFICS'

These well-known engines hardly need further description here. They were built between 1935 and 1938.

1st L.N.E.R. No.	3rd L.N.E.R.* No.	Name
2509	14	Silver Link
2510	15	Quicksilver
2511	16	Silver King
2512	17	Silver Fox
4462	4	Great Snipe/William Whitelaw
4463	18	Sparrow Hawk
4464	19	Bittern
4465	20	Guillemot/Dominion of Pakistan/ Guillemot
4466	6	Herring Gull/Sir Ralph Wedgwood
4467	21	Wild Swan
4468	22	Mallard
4469	—	Gadwall/Sir Ralph Wedgwood
4482	23	Golden Eagle
4483	24	Kingfisher
4484	25	Falcon
4485	26	Kestrel/Miles Beevor
4486	27	Merlin
4487	28	Sea Eagle/Walter K. Whigham
4488	9	Union of South Africa
4489	10	Woodcock/Dominion of Canada
4490	11	Empire of India
4491	12	Commonwealth of Australia
4492	13	Dominion of New Zealand
4493	29	Woodcock

1st L.N.E.R. No.	3rd L.N.E.R.* No.	Name
4494	3	Osprey/Andrew K. McCosh
4495	30	Golden Fleece
4496	8	Golden Shuttle/Dwight D. Eisenhower
4497	31	Golden Plover
4498	7	Sir Nigel Gresley
4499	2	Pochard/Sir Murrough Wilson
4500	1	Garganey/Sir Ronald Matthews
4900	32	Gannet
4901	5	Capercaillie/Charles H. Newton/ Sir Charles Newton
4902	33	Seagull
4903	34	Peregrine/Lord Faringdon

* Like the earlier Pacifics it was at first intended to renumber these in the 500's and 600's, and one or two were actually done. No. 4469 was destroyed in an air raid at York in 1942 and consequently was not included.

The remainder eventually became B.R. 60001–60034 and all were in service until the end of 1962, when the first withdrawals took place.

Four engines have been preserved privately, 'Dwight D. Eisenhower' having gone to the U.S.A. whilst 'Mallard' is in Clapham Museum.

'DIRECTOR' CLASS 4-4-0's CLASS D11

For express working in Scotland over the former N.B.R. lines, Sir Nigel Gresley first adopted the successful G.C.R. Robinson design of 'Director' 4-4-0's, with very slight modifications, twenty-four engines being built by Kitson's in 1924.

Original L.N.E.R. No.	Name	Original L.N.E.R. No.	Name
6378	Bailie MacWheeble	6390	Hobbie Elliott
6379	Baron of Bradwardine	6391	Wizard of the Moor
6380	Evan Dhu	6392	Malcolm Graeme
6381	Flora MacIvor	6393	The Fiery Cross
6382	Colonel Gardiner	6394	Lord James of Douglas
6383	Jonathan Oldbuck	6395	Ellen Douglas
6384	Edie Ochiltree	6396	Maid of Lorn
6385	Luckie Mucklebackit	6397	The Lady of the Lake
6386	Lord Glenallan	6398	Laird of Balmawhapple
6387	Lucy Ashton	6399	Allan Bane
6388	Captain Craigengelt	6400	Roderick Dhu
6389	Haystoun of Bucklaw	6401	James Fitzjames

In 1946 they became 2671–2694, and on Nationalisation 62671–62694. They disappeared between 1958 and 1962.

.W.R. No. 89
'rouville', one
he few named
ines on the
railway.

, 0111 'Vul-
'. Another
.W.R. named
loco.

R. 0-4-0ST
he Master
General'.

One of the s
stud of Isle
Wight Rail
locos, unn
bered, and
tinguished
names on

Southern Region Adams 0-4-4T No. W22.   Under the
enterprising managership of Mr A. B. MacLeod, all
engines in the Isle of Wight, were provided with brass
nameplates.

Owing to the regrettable activities of souvenir h
it had latterly been found necessary to remove
plates for safety. In the Isle of Wight, wooden r
were fitted as here on No. W14.

After the gr
ing all engin
the Isle of W
received na
Stroudley
rier' No. 4 (
14) was a
importation
1930.

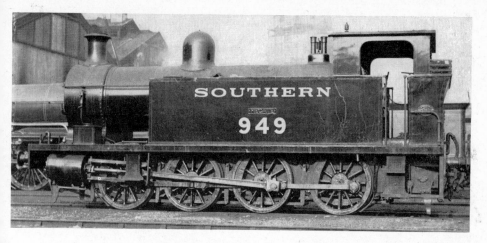

S.R. 0-8-0T No. 949 'Hecate' taken over in 1932 from the Kent and East Sussex Railway.

old L.S.W.R. 2-4-0T at Fort Brockhurst, on the Lee-on-Solent branch train.

The American built 2-4-2T of the Lynton and Barnstaple narrow gauge line.

One of the Brighton 4-6-4T's after conversion to tender engine. These were given names of former locomotive superintendents.

Former Plymouth Devonport and South Western Junction Railway 0-6-2T.

Sister engine to the above, with nameplate mounted in a different position.

Two of the U.S.A. 0-6-0T's purchased by the S.R. in 1947 were latterly used as works shunters at Ashford, and were given names of former S.E. & C.R. locomotive superintendents, 'Wainwright' and 'Maunsell'.

GRESLEY 6′ 8″ 3 CYLINDER 4-4-0's

Built for the North Eastern and Scottish areas of the L.N.E.R., these engines were built between 1927 and 1935. They were of two main varieties, with Walschaert valve gear and with Lentz poppet valves. The Walschaert engines, known as the 'Shires' were named after English and Scottish counties, whilst the poppet valve variety, the 'Hunts', were named after famous hunting packs. (The first two poppet engines, Nos. 336 and 352 at first followed the county naming, but were later renamed to conform). The 'Hunt' engines had a brass model of a fox over the nameplate.

1st L.N.E.R. No.	*1946 No.*	*Name*
201	2736	The Bramham Moor
205	2751	The Albrighton
211	2737	The York and Ainsty
214	2752	The Atherstone
217	2753	The Belvoir
220	2738	The Zetland
222	2754	The Berkeley
226	2755	The Bilsdale
230	2756	The Brocklesby
232	2739	The Badsworth
234	2700	Yorkshire
235	2740	The Bedale
236	2707	Lancashire
238	2757	The Burton
245	2710	Lincolnshire
246	2712	Morayshire
247	2741	The Blankney
249	2713	Aberdeenshire
250	2714	Perthshire
251	2701	Derbyshire
253	2702	Oxfordshire
255	2742	The Braes of Derwent
256	2703	Hertfordshire
258	2758	The Cattistock
264	2704	Stirlingshire
265	2705	Lanarkshire
266	2706	Forfarshire
269	2743	The Cleveland
270	2708	Argyllshire
273	2744	The Holderness
274	2759	The Craven
277	2709	Berwickshire
279	2760	The Cotswold
281	2711	Dumbartonshire
282	2745	The Hurworth
283	2746	The Middleton

G

1st L.N.E.R. No.	*1946 No.*	*Name*
288	2747	The Percy
292	2748	The Southwold
297	2749	The Cottesmore
298	2750	The Pytchley
306	2715	Roxburghshire
307	2716	Kincardineshire
309	2717	Banffshire
310	2718	Kinross-shire
311	2719	Peebles-shire
318	2720	Cambridgeshire
320	2721	Warwickshire
322	2722	Huntingdonshire
327	2723	Nottinghamshire
329	2725	Inverness-shire
335	2724	Bedfordshire
336	2727	Buckinghamshire/The Quorn
352	2726	Leicestershire/The Meynell
353	2761	The Derwent
357	2762	The Fernie
359	2763	The Fitzwilliam
361	2764	The Garth
362	2765	The Goathland
363	2766	The Grafton
364	2767	The Grove
365	2768	The Morpeth
366	2769	The Oakley
368	2770	The Puckeridge
370	2771	The Rufford
374	2772	The Sinnington
375	2773	The South Durham
376	2774	The Staintondale
377	2775	The Tynedale
2753	2728	Cheshire
2754	2729	Rutlandshire
2755	2730	Berkshire
2756	2731	Selkirkshire
2757	2732	Dumfries-shire
2758	2733	Northumberland
2759	2734	Cumberland
2760	2735	Westmorland

No. 365 was rebuilt with two inside cylinders in 1942, but no further engines were so treated. This engine was scrapped in 1952. The whole class became B.R. 62700–62775, and with the exception of the rebuilt 62768, lasted until 1957–1961. No. 246 has been preserved privately.

GRESLEY 6' 8" 4-6-0's 'SANDRINGHAM' CLASS

Built between 1928 and 1937 mainly for work on the Great Eastern section

1st L.N.E.R. No.	*Name*	*1st L.N.E.R. No.*	*Name*
2800	Sandringham	2838	Melton Hall
2801	Holkham	2839	Rendelsham Hall/
2802	Walsingham		Norwich City
2803	Framlingham	2840	Somerleyton Hall
2804	Elveden	2841	Gayton Hall
2805	Burnham Thorpe/	2842	Kilverstone Hall
	Lincolnshire Regiment	2843	Champion Lodge
2806	Audley End	2844	Earlham Hall
2807	Blickling	2845	The Suffolk Regiment
2808	Gunton	2846	Gilwell Park
2809	Quidenham	2847	Helmingham Hall
2810	Honingham Hall	2848	Arsenal
2811	Raynham Hall	2849	Sheffield United
2812	Houghton Hall	2850	Grimsby Town
2813	Woodbastwick Hall	2851	Derby County
2814	Castle Hedingham	2852	Darlington
2815	Culford Hall	2853	Huddersfield Town
2816	Fallodon	2854	Sunderland
2817	Ford Castle	2855	Middlesborough
2818	Wynyard Park	2856	Leeds United
2819	Welbeck Abbey	2857	Doncaster Rovers
2820	Clumber	2858	The Essex Regiment
2821	Hatfield House	2859	Norwich City/East
2822	Alnwick Castle		Anglian
2823	Lambton Castle	2860	Hull City
2824	Lumley Castle	2861	Sheffield Wednesday
2825	Raby Castle	2862	Manchester United
2826	Brancepeth Castle	2863	Everton
2827	Aske Hall	2864	Liverpool
2828	Harewood House	2865	Leicester City
2829	Naworth Castle	2866	Nottingham Forest
2830	Thoresby Park/	2867	Bradford
	Tottenham Hotspur	2868	Bradford City
2831	Serlby Hall	2869	Barnsley
2832	Belvoir Castle/Royal	2870	Manchester City/City
	Sovereign		of London
2833	Kimbolton Castle	2871	Tottenham Hotspur/
2834	Hinchingbrooke		Manchester City/
2835	Milton		Royal Sovereign
2836	Harlaxton Manor	2872	West Ham United
2837	Thorpe Hall		

They became 1600–1672 in 1946 and B.R. 61600–61672 on Nationalisation. In 1937 Nos. 2859 and 2870 were streamlined on the pattern of the A4 'Pacifics' for working the 'East Anglian' express between Norwich and London. One or two of the class were scrapped from 1952 onwards, but most of them lasted until 1958–1960.

GRESLEY 3 CYLINDER 2-8-2's

Six engines built in 1934 and 1936 for the heavy road between Edinburgh and Aberdeen. They were rebuilt in 1943/4 as 4-6-2's.

Original L.N.E.R. No.	1944 No.	1946 No.	Name
2001		501	Cock o' the North
2002		502	Earl Marischal
2003		503	Lord President
2004		504	Mons Meg
2005	994	505	Thane of Fife
2006		506	Wolf of Badenoch

Under the 1944 scheme they would have become 990–995, but only one engine was so renumbered.

They became B.R. 60501–60506 and were scrapped between 1959 and 1961.

GRESLEY 3 CYLINDER 2-6-2's CLASS V2

Built between 1936 and 1944. Only a few of these engines were named:—

Original L.N.E.R. No.	1944 No.	1946 No.	Name
4771		800	Green Arrow
4780	709	809	The Snapper, the East Yorkshire Regiment, The Duke of York's Own
4806		835	The Green Howards, Alexandra, Princess of Wales' Own Yorkshire Regiment
4818		847	St. Peter's School, York A.D. 627
4831		860	Durham School
4843		872	King's Own Yorkshire Light Infantry
4844		873	Coldstreamer
3676		964	The Durham Light Infantry

They became B.R. 60800 etc., and most of them were still in existence at the close of 1962, but the class was by then being withdrawn. The original 'Green Arrow' has been preserved.

THOMPSON MIXED TRAFFIC 4-6-0's CLASS B1

The first series of these engines, built between 1942 and 1947, struck new ground in locomotive nomenclature by being named after various species of South African antelopes. Subsequent engines of this numerous class were in general unnamed, but a few were called after L.N.E.R. directors just prior to Nationalisation.

The first ten came out as 8301–8310, but under the 1946 scheme the class was numbered from 1000 onwards, and the named engines were as follows:—

L.N.E.R. No.	Name	L.N.E.R. No.	Name
1000	Springbok	1030	Nyala
1001	Eland	1031	Reedbuck
1002	Impala	1032	Stembok
1003	Gazelle	1033	Dibatag
1004	Oryx	1034	Chiru
1005	Bongo	1035	Pronghorn
1006	Black Buck	1036	Ralph Assheton
1007	Klipspringer	1037	Jairou
1008	Kudu	1038	Blacktail
1009	Hartebeeste	1039	Steinbok
1010	Wildbeeste	1040	Roedeer
1011	Waterbuck	1189	Sir William Gray
1012	Puku	1215	William Henton Carver
1013	Topi	1221	Sir Alexander
1014	Oribi		Erskine-Hill
1015	Duiker	1237	Geoffrey H. Kitson
1016	Inyala	1238	Leslie Runciman
1017	Bushbuck	1240	Harry Hinchliffe
1018	Gnu	1241	Viscount Ridley
1019	Nilghai	1242	Alexander Reith Gray
1020	Gemsbock	1243	Sir Harold Mitchell
1021	Reitbok	1244	Strang Steel
1022	Sassaby	1245	Murray of Elibank
1023	Hirola	1246	Lord Balfour of Burleigh
1024	Addax	1247	Lord Burghley
1025	Pallah	1248	Geoffrey Gibbs
1026	Ourebi	1249	Fitz Herbert Wright
1027	Madoqua	1250	A. Harold Bibby
1028	Umseke	1251	Oliver Bury
1029	Chamois	61379	Mayflower

The last mentioned engine was built in 1951 after Nationalisation as No. 61379. In addition to its nameplates, two special plaques were fixed on the cab sides in 1952, bearing the following inscription:—"This Locomotive Was Named MAYFLOWER, 13th July, 1951, As A Symbol Of The Ties Binding The Towns Of Boston, And Of The Lasting Friendship Between The U.S.A. And The British Commonwealth."

Scrapping of the B1's on a general scale commenced in 1962.

THOMPSON'S 4-6-2 CLASS A2/1

These four engines, built in 1944, were in effect V2 2-6-2's, but with a leading bogie.

1st L.N.E.R. *No.*	*1946* *No.*	*Name*
3696	507	Highland Chieftain
3697	508	Duke of Rothesay
3698	509	Waverley
3699	510	Robert the Bruce

Under the 1944 scheme they would have become 996-999. As B.R. 60507–60510 they were taken out of service in 1960 and 1961.

GRESLEY 2-6-0's CLASS K4

Original L.N.E.R. *No.*	*1946* *No.*	*Name*
3441	1993	Loch Long
3442	1994	The Great Marquess
3443	1995	Cameron of Locheil
3444	1996	Lord of the Isles
3445	1997	MacCailin Mor
3446	1998	Lord of Dunvegan/MacLeod of MacLeod

Six engines built in 1937/38 for the West Highland line.
They became B.R. 61993–61998, and all were withdrawn in 1961, but No. 3442 has been privately preserved in working order.

GRESLEY 2-6-2 CLASS V4

Sir Nigel Gresley's last design, of which only two were built. They were turned out in 1941, the first one No. 3401 being named 'Bantam Cock'. No. 3402 never bore a name, although it was usually unofficially known as 'Bantam Hen'. They became Nos. 1700 and 1701 in 1947, then B.R. 61700/1 being scrapped in 1957.

THOMPSON PACIFICS, CLASS A2

Built 1946–1948, with sundry modifications between some engines of the series.

500	Edward Thompson	516	Hycilla
511	Airborne	517	Ocean Swell
512	Steady Aim	518	Tehran
513	Dante	519	Honeyway
514	Chamossaire	520	Owen Tudor
515	Sun Stream	521	Watling Street

522	Straight Deal	531	Bahram
523	Sun Castle	60532	Blue Peter
524	Herringbone	60533	Happy Knight
525	A. H. Peppercorn	60534	Irish Elegance
526	Sugar Palm	60535	Hornets Beauty
527	Sun Chariot	60536	Trimbush
528	Tudor Minstrel	60537	Batchelors Button
529	Pearl Diver	60538	Velocity
530	Sayajirao	60539	Bronzino

The last eight came out after Nationalisation and never ran as L.N.E.R engines.

All subsequently became 60500, 60511–60539, and scrapping commenced in 1962.

THOMPSON PACIFICS, CLASS A1

Thompson's express design, built 1948/9. The prototype of this class was No. 60113 'Great Northern', the original G.N.R. Pacific mentioned on page 83. Although none of the subsequent engines ever ran in L.N.E.R. style, they must rank as a design of that Company. They were first turned out un-named, but the names subsequently applied were extremely well chosen, some revived a number of old time names of former locomotives, whilst others commemorate the pre-grouping Companies and some of the locomotive designers thereof.

60114	W. P. Allen	60136	Alcazar
60115	Meg Merrilees	60137	Red Gauntlet
06116	Hal o' the Wynd	60138	Boswell
60117	Bois Roussel	60139	Sea Eagle
60118	Archibald Sturrock	60140	Balmoral
60119	Patrick Stirling	60141	Abbotsford
60120	Kittiwake	60142	Edward Fletcher
60121	Silurian	60143	Sir Walter Scott
60122	Curlew	60144	King's Courier
60123	H. A. Ivatt	60145	Saint Mungo
60124	Kenilworth	60146	Peregrine
60125	Scottish Union	60147	North Eastern
60126	Sir Vincent Raven	60148	Aboyeur
60127	Wilson Wordsell	60149	Amadis
60128	Bongrace	60150	Willbrook
60129	Guy Mannering	60151	Midlothian
60130	Kestrel	60152	Holyrood
60131	Osprey	60153	Flamboyant
60132	Marmion	60154	Bon Accord
60133	Pommern	60155	Borderer
60134	Foxhunter	60156	Great Central
60135	Madge Wildfire	60157	Great Eastern

60158	Aberdonian	60161	North British
60159	Bonnie Dundee	60162	Saint Johnstoun
60160	Auld Reekie		

Withdrawal of this class commenced in 1962.

So far as the L.N.E.R. is concerned, there remains to be mentioned the steam railcars, which were introduced on a considerable scale between 1927 and 1930. They very fittingly bore names of famous stage coaches of the past. Of several varieties, they may be summarised as follows:—

SENTINEL RAILCARS

21	Valiant	244	True Briton
22	Brilliant	250	Rob Roy
26	Tally Ho	253	Red Rover
29	Rockingham	254	Phoenix
210	High Flyer	255	Perseverance
212	Eclipse	263	North Star
220	Water Witch	265	Neptune
225	True Blue	267	Liberty
226	Ebor	272	Hero
237	Rodney	273	Trafalgar
238	Yorkshire Hussar	283	Teazle
2133/35	Nettle	310	Prince Regent
2133	Cleveland	311/31073	Quicksilver
2135	Integrity	312	Retaliator
2136	Hope	51912	Rising Sun
2139	Hark Forward	51913	Rival
2140	Eagle	51914	Royal Forrester
2144	Traveller	2198	Times
2145	Ruby	2200	Surprise
2147	Woodpecker	2217	Royal Charlotte
2151	Umpire	2218	Telegraph
2152	Courrier	2219	New Fly
31	Flower of Yarrow	2231	Swift
45/43301	Commerce	2232	Alexander
51908	Expedition	220	Defence
51909	Waterloo	246	Royal Sovereign
32	Fair Maid	248	Tantivy
33/71/33	Highland Chieftain	2235	Britannia
34	Tweedside	2236	British Queen
36	Royal Eagle	2238	Celerity
37	Clydesdale	2242	Cornwallis
38	Pearl	2245	Criterion
39	Protector	2257	Defiance

2261	Diligence	2279	Norfolk
2267	Recovery	313	Banks of Don
2268	Emerald	314	Queen of Beauty
2270	Independent	2281	Old John Bull
2271	Industry	2283	Old Blue
2276/31070/2276	North Briton	2291	Phenomena

All of the above were withdrawn from service during the 1940's.

CLAYTON RAILCARS

2121/41/2121	Pilot	2110	Comet
285	Rapid	2120/42/43302	Chevy Chase
287	Royal Sailor	2122/43/43303	Railway
289	Wellington	2130/44/43304	Bang Up
296	Wonder	61999/43305	Transit
2101	Union		

These were scrapped during the later 1930's. All of the railcars were numbered in the coaching stock list and renumbering occurred when they were transferred from one area to another.

There were also some experimental diesel railcars.

25	Tyneside Venturer	224	Lady Hamilton	232	Northumbrian

Midland and Great Northern Joint Railway

As an eventual constituent of the L.N.E.R., the M. & G.N.J.R. should be fittingly included at this stage, but it only possessed two named engines of minor importance.These were a couple of small Hudswell Clarke 0-4-0ST's dating from 1878 and 1880.

4A	Alpha	5A	Vici

'Alpha' was sold in 1920, and 'Vici' was out of service in Melton Constable yard for several years until it finally disappeared about 1930.

Mention should also be made however of a series of pretty little 4-4-0T's built between 1878 and 1881 for the Lynn and Fakenham Railway. This line was absorbed by the Eastern and Midlands Railway, which concern in turn became the M. & G.N.J.R. in 1893. On the E. & M.R. and M. & G.N.J.R. numbers were as follows, but the names were removed by the Eastern and Midlands.

8	Hillington	19	Great Yarmouth	31/40	Martham
9	Fakenham	20	Kings Lynn	32/41	North Walsham
10	Norwich				

The later history of this class is interesting. Between 1906 and 1912 Nos. 8, 10, 19, and 40 worked on the Midland Railway and were repainted in that

Company's red livery. They were adapted for motor working with Pullman cars and renumbered respectively 2, 5, 1, and 10 to correspond with the vehicles to which they were permanently attached. They were sold to the Government during the first world war, and No. 10 turned up on the Longmoor Military Railway, where it received the name 'Kingsley' (see page 161). It survived as late as 1946, although for many years it had only been used for deliberate derailing and re-railing practice. Of the others, No. 41 was scrapped in 1904, but Nos. 9 and 20 became M. & G.N.R. 9A and 20A, and were not broken up until the early 1930's.

Metropolitan Railway

Most of the steam engines of the Metropolitan Railway were transferred to L.N.E.R. in 1937, although a few were retained by the London Transport Board for departmental duties. One class of the 'main line' engines, was named, a set of four 0-6-4T's built in 1915.

Met. No.	1st L.N.E.R. No.	1946 L.N.E.R. No.	Name
94	6154	(9075)	Lord Aberconway
95	6155	9076	Robert H. Selbie
96	6156	9077	Charles Jones
97	6157	—	Brill

No. 6157 had been scrapped in 1943 and 6154 went in 1946 without receiving its new number. The other two lasted until 1948. The Metropolitan's fine electric locomotives became the property of the London Transport Board, at the same time. These were as follows:—

1	John Lyon	11	George Romney
2	Oliver Cromwell/Thomas Lord	12	Sarah Siddons
3	Sir Ralph Verney	13	Dick Whittington
4	Lord Byron	14	Benjamin Disraeli
5	John Hampden	15	Wembley 1924
6	William Penn	16	Oliver Goldsmith
7	Edmund Burke	17	Florence Nightingale
8	Sherlock Holmes	18	Michael Faraday
9	John Milton	19	John Wycliffe
10	William Ewart Gladstone/ W. E. Gladstone	20	Sir Christopher Wren

The original Metropolitan nameplates were of a very handsome ornamental design, but they were all removed for their metal scrap value at the beginning of the second world war. In 1953 it was decided to restore the names of the locomotives still in service, but Nos. 15, 17, 19, and 20 had meanwhile been scrapped, and No. 9 never had its name replaced. Also 'Oliver Cromwell' was renamed, and that of No. 10 altered. The new nameplates were smaller than the old ones and much plainer in design. With the extension of the electrification to Amersham in 1960 through working of multiple unit electrics became possible, and the engines were consequently taken out of ordinary service, but Nos. 1, 3, 5 and 12 were kept for departmental duties.

One or two other odd engines had been acquired by the Metropolitan earlier in the century; these were Manning Wardle 0-6-0ST's. One of them was named 'Nellie', and there were three others which had worked on the Oxford and Aylesbury Tramway (which line never reached further than the small village of Brill, in Buckinghamshire), these being:—

Huddersfield No. 1   Brill No. 2/No. 1   Wotton No. 2

They were later superseded by standard Metropolitan 4-4-0T's on the branch and scrapped.

IV
The Southern Group
London and South Western Railway

The South Western had abandoned naming its express engines when Mr
William Adams replaced W. G. Beattie as locomotive superintendent in 1878.
The few exceptions which occurred after that date were surprisingly enough
all tank engines, some of which were acquired from Southampton Docks. The
latter were all of the 0-4-0ST variety, and may be summarised as follows:—

L.S.W.R. Nos.	Name	
108,0108	Cowes	Disappeared 1914–1916.
109,0109	Southampton	No. 0110 was sold to Kynochs
110,0110	Ritzbuttel	of Birmingham.
111,0111	Vulcan	Sold 1924
392,0392	Lady Portsmouth	Sold 1914
408,0408	Bretwalda	Sold 1926
457,734	Clausentum	Scrapped 1945
458,0458,3458		
B.R. 30458	Ironside	Scrapped 1954

There was also a survival from the Beattie era, a 2-4-0T No. 21 (later 021)
'Scott', which survived until 1909.

The taking over of Southampton Docks in 1892 necessitated the construction
of new engines for shunting purposes between 1891 and 1896, and Mr Adams
turned out a series of twenty 0-4-0T's, twelve of which were allocated to the
Docks, and given names, as under:—

L.S.W.R. No.	Name	L.S.W.R. No.	Name
81	Jersey	95	Honfleur
85	Alderney	96	Normandy
86	Havre	97	Brittany
89	Trouville	98	Cherbourg
90	Caen	102	Granville
93	St. Malo	176	Guernsey

Two further engines were constructed by Mr Drummond in 1908.
746   later 101   Dinan   747   later 147   Dinard

All of the above worked in Southampton Docks until 1947, when a series of fourteen U.S.A. 0-6-0T's were purchased by the S.R., and the older engines mostly sent elsewhere, although one or two remained at the docks until quite recently. Latterly the survivors lost their names and by the end of 1962 only one or two remained. Nos. 86–89, 93, 94, 96 and 102 survived to have 30000 added to their numbers in B.R. stock.

Between 1889 and 1895 Mr Adams brought out a series of 0-4-4T's with 4' 10" wheels which eventually became familiar all over the system and formed an extremely useful class which performed all manner of miscellaneous duties from shunting to local passenger trains. They were numbered 177–236. In 1890 No. 185 was temporarily named 'Alexandra' when working a Royal Train over the newly opened Bisley Camp branch. It was not however until after the grouping that a considerable number of these engines were sent over by the S.R. to the Isle of Wight where they quickly replaced the older independent Companies' locomotives, and were latterly the only class of locomotive to be found in the Island. All were renumbered and given names on transfer, the complete list being as follows:—

L.S.W.R. No.	*I. of W. No.*	*Name*
178	W14	Fishbourne
195	W15	Cowes
217	W16	Ventnor
208	W17	Seaview
220	W18	Ningwood
206	W19	Osborne
211	W20	Shanklin
205	W21	Sandown
215	W22	Brading
188	W23	Totland
209	W24	Calbourne
190	W25	Godshill
210	W26	Whitwell
184	W27	Merstone
186	W28	Ashey
202	W29	Alverstone
219	W30	Shorwell
180	W31	Chale
226	W32	Bonchurch
218	W33	Bembridge
201	W34	Newport
181	W35	Freshwater
198	W36	Carisbrooke

Nos. 15, 19, 23 and 34 were scrapped in 1955–6 following closure of some of the branches, but many still remained in service until the end of 1966, when steam working in the Island came to an end.

The last express passenger engines built for the L.S.W.R. were a series of

2-cylinder 4-6-0's built by Mr Urie between 1918 and 1923, which were the forerunners of the famous 'King Arthur' class of 1925.

When the latter appeared the original L.S.W.R. engines were incorporated into the class and given names associated with the Knights of the Round Table, as under:—

736	Excalibur	746	Pendragon
737	King Uther	747	Elaine
738	King Pellinore	748	Vivien
739	King Leodegrance	749	Iseult
740	Merlin	750	Morgan le Fay
741	Joyous Gard	751	Etarre
742	Camelot	752	Linette
743	Lyonesse	753	Melisande
744	Maid of Astolat	754	The Green Knight
745	Tintagel	755	The Red Knight

At Nationalisation they became B.R. 30736–30755 and were taken out of service between 1953 and 1958.

These names have since been transferred to B.R. standard class 5 4-6-0's Nos. 73080–73089 and 73110–73119, although not in the same order (see page 131).

South Eastern and Chatham Railway

The S.E. & C.R. was incorporated in 1899 by the amalgamation of two long standing rivals, the South Eastern and the London, Chatham and Dover. Neither of these lines had gone in for naming its locomotives to any extent in fact the S.E.R. hardly at all. The L.C. & D.R. however, had named most of its passenger engines and a few of its tanks at an earlier period, and one of the latter actually lasted to carry its name into S. E. & C.R. days. This was a 0-4-2WT, one of a series of six built by Neilson's in 1873. This engine, 'Scotia', was numbered 100 in the S.E. & C.R. list, and at the amalgamation became S. E. & C.R. No. 559. There is in existence a photograph taken in 1901 which shows it to be then running as No. 559 'Scotia' and as such it was undoubtedly the only S.E. & C.R. engine ever to bear a name during the existence of the Company, as the rest of the class had lost theirs by the time they acquired their new identity.

There was however one new engine of the old South Eastern Railway which carried a name for a time, one of Mr J. Stirling's 7' 0" 4-4-0's No. 240, built in 1889 and sent to the Paris Exhibition in that year, for which occasion it was given the name 'Onward'. It probably only carried it for a short time, and had almost certainly lost it by the time it came into S.E. & C.R. stock.

From thence until absorption into the S.R. in 1923 no S.E. & C.R. engine ever bore a name, although two of its engines did acquire names subsequent to the grouping. The first of these was Mr Maunsell's original 2-6-4T No. 790, turned out in 1917, and the only one of its class until further examples were built by the S. R. in 1925, whereupon No. 790 was christened 'River Avon'.

As these engines were more essentially a S.R. class, further consideration of No. 790 can best be dealt with under that heading (see page 126).

Then there was No. 763, one of Mr Wainwright's final class of 4-4-0, built in 1914. During the General Strike in 1926 the volunteer driver and fireman who were running the engine christened it 'Betty Baldwin' in very well executed lettering on the front splashers. Although the naming was of course quite unofficial it was so well done, and moreover lasted for several months until the engine next went into shops for overhaul and repaint that it now merits inclusion in this record.

London Brighton and South Coast Railway

At the turn of the century, the L.B. & S.C.R. possessed by far the greatest proportion of named locomotives of any major railway, unless one includes the London, Tilbury and Southend, with its much smaller locomotive stock (see page 66). Although its comparatively modest total of 600 odd engines could not quite compare with the thousand or two of the largest Companies, its percentage of named engines was considerably the highest of any of the principal railways until Mr D. Earle Marsh came on the scene in 1905 and proceeded to remove most of the names that had been bestowed under the Stroudley regime.

The method of applying names on the L.B. & S.C.R. in those days was in the form of handsome hand painted lettering, bestowed, in the case of tank engines, in the obvious position of the tank sides, and with tender engines on the usual place on the driving wheel splashers. The fact that in 1900 the only engines which were not distinguished by the addition of names were the 0-6-0 freight engines of Stroudley and Billinton (the 'Vulcans') designs seems rather to point to the fact that on these particular engines the splasher—the only practicable place for a name—was simply not large enough for the purpose.

It will be noticed that many of the names chosen—particularly on the tank classes—were place names in Brighton territory, and eventually there could hardly have been a hamlet or village in Surrey and Sussex whose name was not emblazoned on the striking yellow tank sides of one of the Brighton Company's engines. Whether this ever led to confusing would-be passengers, as had been found on the Great Western, is not recorded, but it is doubtful whether this was the cause of Mr Marsh's decision to dename the engines.

The earliest class to be considered is the well known 'Terrier' tank of 1872, of which fifty were constructed between that year and 1880. That they are nowadays so well known lies probably in the fact that the few survivors were the oldest engines in the service of British Railways.

The original names and numbers are as follows:—

35	Morden	39	Denmark
36	Bramley	40	Brighton
37	Southdown	41	Piccadilly
38	Millwall	42	Tulse Hill

43	Gipsy Hill	64	Kemp Town
44	Fulham	65	Tooting
45	Merton	66	Hatcham
46	Newington	67	Brixton
47	Cheapside	68	Clapham
48	Leadenhall	69	Peckham
49	Bishopsgate	70	Poplar
50	Whitechapel	71	Wapping
51	Rotherhithe	72	Fenchurch
52	Surrey	73	Deptford
53	Ashtead	74	Shadwell
54	Waddon	75	Blackwall
55	Stepney	76	Hailsham
56	Shoreditch	77	Wonersh
57	Thames	78	Knowle
58	Wandle	79	Minories
59	Cheam	80	Bookham
60	Ewell	81	Beulah
61	Sutton	82	Boxhill
62	Martello	83	Earlswood
63	Preston	84	Crowborough

The subsequent history of this class is somewhat complex, many having been sold out of service, although some of them were scrapped as long ago as 1901. The few survivors in B.R. stock in 1962 have long since ceased to carry names. Two which were sold to the Kent and East Sussex Railway are detailed on page 161, three others went to the Shropshire and Montgomery and some to the Isle of Wight, both before and after the grouping, the latter being eventually named under Southern Railway auspices as detailed on page 124.

No. 82 'Boxhill' has been restored to its L.B. & S.C.R. livery and is now in Clapham Museum whilst several others have been preserved under private auspices.

STROUDLEY 0-4-2T's CLASS D

A numerous class constructed by Mr Stroudley between 1873 and 1887 for surburban work.

1	Sydenham	11	Selhurst
2	Wandsworth	12	Wallington
3	Battersea	13	Pimlico
4	Mickleham	14	Chelsea
5	Streatham	15	Brompton
6	Wimbledon	16	Silverdale
7	Bermondsey	17	Dulwich
8	Brockley	18	Stockwell
9	Anerley	19	Belmont
10	Banstead	20	Carshalton

Maunsell's 4-cylinder 4-6-0 'Lord Nelson'.

Type of nameplate as applied to the 'King Arthur' class.

Maunsell's 'Schools' class No. 904, 'Lancing'.

S.R. Pacific 'Battle of Britain' class No. 34051.

Bulleid 'Merchant Navy' class No. 35011.

B.R. class 5 'Morgan le The namepla placed on running pla position diff to get at to clean, with result that t plates usu get dirty somewhat in spicuous

B.R. 'Britar class 'Iron D with pair name, the or al plates ha been remove a safety caution aga pilfering

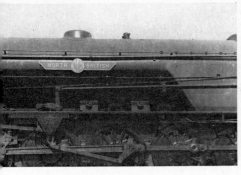

. 'Austerity' 2-10-0 No. 90774. No. 90773 was also named 'North British'.

W.D. 'Austerity' 2-8-0 No. 90732, the only one to carry a name.

B.R. 'Britannia' class No. 70050.

Nameplate on electric locomotive No. 26051.

R. Western Region diesel No. D813. This class s nameplates with lettering after the old G.W.R. style.

The plainer type of nameplate as applied to the later Western Region diesels.

Metropolitan Railway, Oxford and Aylesbury Tramroad loco.

Metropolitan Railway electric loco No. 8, showing the original type of nameplates which were removed for scrap during the war and later replaced by a plainer design.

Metropolitan Railway 0-6-4T No. 96.

21	Beddington		252	Buckhurst
22	Addington		253	Pelham
23	Mayfield		254	Hambledon
24	Brambletye		255	Willingdon
25	Rotherfield		256	Stanford
26	Hartfield		257	Brading
27	Uckfield		258	Cosham
28	Isfield		259	Telford/Barnham
29	Lambeth		260	Lavington
30	Camberwell		261	Wigmore
31	Borough		262	Oxted
32	Walworth		263	Purley
33	Mitcham		264	Langston
34	Balham		265	Chipstead
35	Southwark		266	Charlwood
36	New Cross		267	Maresfield
221	Warbleton		268	Baynards
222	Cuckmere		269	Crawley
223	Balcombe		270	Warnham
224	Crowhurst		271	Eridge
225	Ashburne		272	Nevill/Goring
226	Westham		273	Dornden
227	Heathfield		274	Guildford
228	Seaford		275	Cranleigh
229	Dorking		276	Rudgwick
230	Brookhouse		277	Slinfold
231	Horsham		278	Groombridge
232	Lewes		279	Tunbridge Wells
233	Handcross		280	Grinstead
234	Rottingdean		281	Withyham
235	Broadwater		282	Rowfant
236	Ardingly		283	Aldgate
237	Cuckfield		284	Ashburnham
238	Lindfield		285	Holmwood
239	Patcham		286	Ranmore
240	Ditchling		287	Buryhill
241	Stanmer		288	Effingham
242	Ringmer		289	Holmbury
243	Ovingdean		290	Denbies
244	Hassocks		291	Deepdene
245	Withdean		292	Leigham
246	Bramber		293	Norbury
247	Arlington		294	Rosebery/Falmer
248	Ashurst		295	Whippingham
249	Hilsea		296	Osborne/Peckham
250	Hoathly		297	Bonchurch
251	Singleton		298	Southwark

H

299	New Cross		357	Riddlesdown
351	Chailey		358	Henfield
352	Lavant		359	Egmont
353	Keymer		360	Leconfield
354	Lancing		361	Upperton
355	Worthing		362	Kidbrooke
356	Coulsdon			

All lost their names from 1905 onwards, and a certain amount of renumbering took place. The last in service was No. 2252 (formerly 252 'Buckhurst') withdrawn in 1950.

The last survivor of all was No. 357, sold to the Whittingham Asylum Railway (see page 174).

STROUDLEY 0-6-0T's CLASS E

A class introduced in 1874 for general shunting and light freight work, but also used on occasions on passenger trains.

85	Cannes		114	Trouville
86	Geneva		115	Lorraine
87	Bologna		116	Touraine
88	Rhine		117	Florence
89	Brest		118	Trocadero
90	Berne		119	Rochelle
91	Fishbourne		120	Provence
92	Polesden		121	Verona
93	Calbourne		122	Leghorn
94	Shorwell		123	Seine
95	Luccombe		124	Bayonne
96	Salzberg		125	Navarre
97	Honfleur		126	Gascony
98	Marseilles		127	Poitiers
99	Bordeaux		128	Avignon
100	Calvados		129	Alençon
101	Orleans		130	Rennes
102	Cherbourg		131	Gournay
103	Normandy		132	Epernay
104	Brittany		133	Picardy
105	Morlaix		134	Ancona
106	Guernsey		135	Foligno
107	Alderney		136	Brindisi
108	Jersey		137	Dijon
109	Strasbourg		138	Macon
110	Burgundy		139	Lombardy
111	Montpellier		140	Toulouse
112	Versailles		141	Mentone
113	Granville/Durdans		142	Toulon

143	Nuremburg	150	Adriatic
144	Chambery	151	Helvetia
145	France	152	Hungary
146	Havre	153	Austria
147	Danube	154	Madrid
148	Vienna	155	Brenner
149	Lucerne	156	Munich

The names were all removed by Mr D. Earle Marsh, but four of the engines were transferred to the Isle of Wight in the 1930's and acquired new names (see page 122). Another similar engine but with enlarged dimensions was built in 1884, No. 157 'Barcelona'. This was broken up in 1922.

A further six engines, slightly modified by R. J. Billinton, were turned out in 1891:—

159	Edenbridge	162	Southwater
160	Portslade	163	Southwick
161	Aldrington	164	Spithead

The last of the E class 0-6-0T's was withdrawn in 1962.

With all these classes just described, the 'Terriers', D1's and E1's, a certain amount of renumbering had taken place in Brighton days, mostly into the 600's, which series at that time formed a sort of duplicate list for older engines due for replacement (although in actual fact many of them were destined long to outlive the newer engines which had acquired their original numbers.)

The majority of classes D1 and E1, and also quite a number of Terriers had 2000 added to their numbers at the grouping, and those that survived Nationalisation were again altered by being increased by 30000, but no engines of class D1 actually lasted long enough to be renumbered thus.

STROUDLEY 2-2-2 ENGINES BUILT BETWEEN 1874 AND 1882

151 (later 326)	Grosvenor	339	London
327	Imberhorne	340	Medina
328	Sutherland	341	Parkhurst
329	Stephenson	342	St. Lawrence
330	Newhaven	343	Wilmington
331	Fairlight	344	Hurstmonceux
332	Shanklin	345	Plumpton
333	Ventnor	346	Alfriston
334	Petworth	347	Dallington
335	Connaught	348	Lullington
336	Edinburgh	349	Albany
337	Yarmouth	350	Southbourne
338	Bembridge		

The last survivor, 'Stephenson', worked until 1914.

STROUDLEY MIXED TRAFFIC 0-4-2's

6' 2" driving wheels, built 1876 and 1883.

300	Lyons	307	Venice
301	Caen	308	Como
302	Turin	309	Splugen
303	Milan	310	Laval
304	Nice	311	Rhone
305	Genoa	312	Albion
306	Naples	313	Paris

All were scrapped during the early years of the century.

STROUDLEY EXPRESS 0-4-2's 6' 6" WHEELS

These engines were the forerunners of the better known 'Gladstone's' detailed in the next section.

208	Richmond	211	Beaconsfield/Cavendish
209	Devonshire	212	Hartington
210	Cornwall/Belgravia	213	Norfolk

These engines eventually became Nos. 608–613, but did not enjoy a long life, all being scrapped between 1901 and 1904.

STROUDLEY EXPRESS 0-4-2's 6' 6" WHEELS

The very successful 'Gladstone' class were built between 1882 and 1891 thirty-six engines in all as under:—

172	Littlehampton	190	Arthur Otway
173	Cottesloe	191	Gordon-Lennox
174	Fratton	192	Jacomb-Hood
175	Hayling	193	Fremantle
176	Pevensey	194	Bickersteth
177	Southsea	195	Cardew
178	Leatherhead	196	Ralph L. Lopes
179	Sandown	197	Jonas Levy
180	Arundel	198	Sheffield
181	Croydon	199	Samuel Laing
182	Hastings	200	Beresford
183	Eastbourne	214	Gladstone
184	Carew D. Gilbert/ Stroudley	215	Salisbury
185	George A. Wallis	216	Granville
186	De la Warr	217	Northcote
187	Philip Rose	218	Beaconsfield
188	Allen Sarle	219	Cleveland
189	Edward Blount	220	Hampden

Under Marsh's regime all lost their names with the exception of Nos. 173, 184, 190, 199 and 214 which for some reason were allowed to retain theirs until Southern days, when they became nameless.

Ten of these engines were scrapped prior to the first world war, but the remaining 26 were kept in service for a considerable time longer, and No. 172 was not taken out of traffic until 1933. Nos. 214, 217, and 219 latterly ran as Nos. 618, 620 and 619 respectively.

The prototype engine 'Gladstone' was restored to its original condition as No. 214 after withdrawal in 1927 and is now preserved.

BILLINTON 0-6-2T's CLASS E4

The original engine, No. 158, was designed by Stroudley, but did not appear until 1891 after his death. The class eventually comprised the following engines, built between 1891 and 1903.

158	West Brighton	494	Woodgate
463	Wivelsfield	495	Chessington
464	Woodmancote	496	Chiddingfold
465	Hurst Green	497	Donnington
466	Honor Oak	498	Strettington
467	Berwick	499	Woodendean
468	Midhurst	500	Puttenham
469	Beachy Head	501	Stoat's Nest
470	East Hoathly	502	Ridgewood
471	Forest Hill	503	Buckland
472	Fay Gate	504	Chilworth
473	Birch Grove	505	Annington
474	Bletchingly	506	Catherington
475	Partridge Green	507	Horley
476	Beeding	508	Bognor
477	Poynings	509	Southover
478	Newick	510	Twineham
479	Bevendean	511	Lingfield
480	Fletching	512	Kingswood
481	Itchingfield	513	Densworth
482	Newtimber	514	Barcombe
483	Hellingly	515	Swanmore
484	Hackbridge	516	Rustington
485	Ashington	517	Limpsfield
486	Godalming	518	Porchester
487	Fishergate	519	Portfield
488	Oakwood	520	Westbourne
489	Boxgrove	556	Tadworth
490	Bohemia	557	Northlands
491	Hangleton	558	Chiltington
492	Jevington	559	Framfield
493	Telscombe	560	Pembury

561	Walberton	577	Blackstone
562	Laughton	578	Horsebridge
563	Wineham	579	Roehampton
564	Nettlestone	580	Shermanbury
565	Littleton	581	Warningcamp
566	Durrington	582	Horndean

All of these lasted into S.R. days, although the original 'West Brighton' was scrapped in 1934 without receiving its allotted number 2158. The remainder all became S.R. 2463, etc., and practically all survived into B.R. stock as 32463 etc., a small handful still being in service at the close of 1962. All had of course long since lost their names in Brighton days.

Early in 1963 No. 473 was sold to the Bluebell Railway and had its old name restored (see page 155).

BILLINTON 0-6-2T's CLASS E3

Similar to class E4, but with a 4' 6" driving wheel in place of 5' 0".

165	Blatchington	455	Brockhurst
166	Cliftonville	456	Aldingbourne
167	Saddlescombe	457	Wartersfield
168	Southborough	458	Chalvington
169	Bedhampton	459	Warlingham
170	Bishopstone	460	Warminghurst
453	Broadbridge	461	Staplefield
454	Storrington	462	Washington

The history of these engines is similar to class E4, but all had gone by 1959.

BILLINTON 0-6-2T's CLASS E5

A larger class of 0-6-2T with 5' 6" wheels for semi express work, built between 1902 and 1904.

399	Middleton	574	Copthorne
400	Winchelsea	575	Westergate
401	Woldingham	576	Brenchley
402	Wanborough	583	Handcombe
403	Fordcombe	584	Lordington
404	Hardham	585	Crowborough
405	Fernhurst	586	Maplehurst
406	Colworth	587	Brighton
567	Freshwater	588	Hawkesbury
568	Carisbrooke	589	Ambersham
569	Kensington	590	Lodsworth
570	Armington	591	Tillington
571	Hickstead	592	Eastergate
572	Farncombe	593	Hollington
573	Nutbourne	594	Shortbridge

As with other tank classes, Mr Marsh removed the names from these engines as they went through the shops, and acquired his chocolate brown livery, but three engines of this particular class managed to retain the Stroudley yellow and their names for a considerable time, Nos. 399 'Middleton', 406 'Colworth', and 591 'Tillington', which were all still running thus at least until 1914 and in fact 'Tillington' was not finally repainted until as late as 1917.

All became S.R. 2399 etc., and most of them survived until Nationalisation as B.R. 32399, etc., the last being taken out of service in 1956.

BILLINTON 0-6-2T's CLASS E6

A freight version of class E5, with 4' 6" wheels. Twelve engines were constructed in 1904 and 1905, but the last four were built after Mr Marsh's accession, and consequently never bore names.

407	Worplesdon	411	Blackheath
408	Binderton	412	Tandridge
409	Graffham	413	Fenchurch
410	Chilgrove	414	Piccadilly

They duly became S.R. 2407 and B.R. 32407 etc., and four of them were still running at the end of 1962

BILLINTON 0-4-4T's CLASS D3

36 engines built 1892–1896.

363	Goldsmid/Havant	381	Fittleworth
364	Truscott	382	Farlington
365	Victoria	383	Three Bridges
366	Crystal Palace	384	Cooksbridge
367	Norwood	385	Portsmouth
368	Newport	386	Chichester
369	Burgess Hill	387	Steyning
370	Haywards Heath	388	Emsworth
371	Angmering	389	Shoreham
372	Amberley	390	St. Leonards
373	Billingshurst	391	Drayton
374	Pulborough	392	Polegate
375	Glynde	393	Woodside
376	Folkington	394	Cowfold
377	Hurstpierpoint	395	Gatwick
378	Horsted Keynes	396	Clayton
379	Sanderstead	397	Bexhill
380	Thornton Heath	398	Haslemere

As with the other tank classes, all lost their names from 1905 onwards. The last in service was B.R. 32390, withdrawn in 1955.

BILLINTON 4-4-0's CLASS B2

Built 1895–1898.

171	Nevill	213	Bessemer
201	Rosebery	314	Charles C. Macrae
202	Trevithick	315	Duncannon/J. Gay
203	Henry Fletcher	316	Goldsmid
204	Telford	317	Gerald Loder
205	Hackworth	318	Rothschild
206	Smeaton	319	John Fowler/Leconfield
207	Brunel	320	Rastrick
208	Abercorn	321	John Rennie
209	Wolfe Barry	322	G. P. Bidder
210	Fairbairn	323	William Cubitt
211	Whitworth	324	John Hawkshaw
212	Armstrong		

Marsh removed all of the names from 1905 onwards except those of Nos. 213, 315 and 319, which retained them until Southern days. All were scrapped by 1933.

BILLINTON 4-4-0's CLASS B4

An enlarged version of class B2, built 1899–1902.

42	His Majesty	59	Baden Powell
43	Duchess of Fife	60	Kimberley
44	Cecil Rhodes	61	Ladysmith
45	Bessborough	62	Mafeking
46	Prince of Wales	63	Pretoria
47	Canada	64	Windsor/Norfolk
48	Australia	65	Sandringham
49	Queensland/Duchess of Norfolk	66	Balmoral/Billinton
50	Tasmania	67	Osborne
51	Wolferton	68	Marlborough
52	Siemens/Sussex	69	Bagshot
53	Sirdar/Richmond	70	Holyrood/Devonshire
54	Empress/La France/Empress/ Princess Royal	71	Goodwood
55	Emperor	72	Sussex
56	Roberts	73	Westminster
57	Buller	74	Cornwall
58	Kitchener		

As with class B2, most of the names were removed from 1905 onwards, but again a few were allowed to retain theirs, these being Nos. 42, 46, 52–54, 64, 66, and 70. All lost them however at the grouping. Twelve of the engines were reconstructed in 1922 and 1923 as class B4x, and No. 52 'Sussex' actually ran in rebuilt form still carrying its name for a short time. The last engines were taken out of service in 1951.

MARSH'S 'ATLANTICS' CLASSES H1 AND H2

Marsh built two series of Atlantics, Nos. 37–41 in 1905/6 and Nos. 421–426 in 1911/12. All were turned out unnamed, and remained so in Brighton days with the exception of No. 39, which became 'La France' in 1909, when it was employed to work a train carrying the President of France to Victoria. It retained this name until the grouping.

In 1925 the Southern decided to name the whole class, and they duly became as follows:—

37	Selsey Bill	421	South Foreland
38	Portland Bill	422	North Foreland
39	Hartland Point	423	The Needles
40	St. Catherine's Point	424	Beachy Head
41	Peveril Point	425	Trevose Head
		426	St. Alban's Head

In accordance with S.R. practice, nameplates were provided. In Brighton days, all names had been applied by hand painting. They later became 2037–2041 and 2421–2426 but only 2037–2039 of the first batch survived into B.R. days, and 32039 was the only one to carry its B.R. no. This engine had been used for experimental purposes by Mr Bulleid in connection with the building of his 'Leader' class. These three engines were scrapped in 1951, but five of the later lot, as Nos. 32421/2, and 32424–6 survived until 1956–8, No. 32424 being the last 'Atlantic' engine to run in the country.

BILLINTON 4-6-2T's BUILT 1910/12

325	Abergavenny	326	Bessborough

These engines lost their names at the grouping. As S.R. 2325/6 and B.R. 32325/6 they survived until 1951.

BILLINTON 4-6-4T's

Seven engines, Nos. 327–333 were built between 1914 and 1922, but only three of these were at first named.

327	Charles C. Macrae	329	Stephenson	333	Remembrance

No. 329 took the name formerly borne by the earlier Stroudley 2-2-2 No. 329, whilst No. 333 was the Brighton's War Memorial engine and carried a commemorative plate to that effect.

After the Brighton and Eastbourne electrification there was no suitable work for these fine locomotives and they were therefore rebuilt as 4-6-0 tender engines, No. 329 and 333 retaining their names, and the others acquiring new ones, commemorating early locomotive designers in the same way as 329, the class then being as follows:—

2327	Trevithick	2331	Beattie
2328	Hackworth	2332	Stroudley
2329	Stephenson	2333	Remembrance
2330	Cudworth		

New semi circular plates to fit the splashers had to be cast in place of the oblong ones hitherto carried by 'Stephenson' and 'Remembrance' since the grouping (they had previously had painted names in accordance with L.B. & S.C.R. practice) but the last mentioned engine had its War Memorial plate duly transferred.

As B.R. Nos. 32327–32333 they ran until 1951–1957.

Lynton and Barnstaple Railway

This narrow gauge line, which closed in 1935, possessed four engines at the grouping in 1923, a fifth being added by the S.R. in 1925. They were un-numbered in L. & B.R. days.

One engine was a 2-4-2T of American design, having been built by Baldwins in 1900. This became No. 762 in the S.R. and was named 'Lyn'.

The other engines were 2-6-2T's built by Manning Wardle as under:—

S.R. Nos.	Names	S.R. Nos.	Names
759	Yeo	761	Taw
760	Exe	188	Lew

The last mentioned was of course strictly speaking a S.R. engine, but is most conveniently dealt with under this heading. This engine was sold to some new owners in Brazil when the line was closed, the other locomotives being broken up.

Plymouth, Devonport and South Western Junction Railway

This small independent line possessed three engines at the time of the grouping, two 0-6-2T's and a 0-6-0T (No. 3). Although never actually owned by the L.S.W.R., they nevertheless were at first repainted in L.S.W.R. colours as no decision was made as to the style of painting to be adopted by the S.R. until several months after the amalgamation.

P.D. & S.W.J. No.	L.S.W.R. No.	B.R. No.	Name	
3	756	(30756) not carried	A. S. Harris	Withdrawn 1951
4	757	30757	Earl of Mount Edgecumbe	Withdrawn 1957
5	758	30758	Earl St. Levan	Withdrawn 1956

Isle of Wight Railway

This small line, the most important of the three independent systems which served the Isle of Wight until 1923, did not number its locomotives.

The 'main line' fleet, and hard worked engines they were, too, consisted of seven 2-4-0T's which had been built by Beyer Peacock between 1864 and 1883. The S.R. gave numbers in their special list to all of them except one, which was considered too worn out to warrant further service.

S.R. No.	Name	S.R. No.	Name
W13	Ryde	W16	Wroxall
—	Sandown	W17	Brading
W14	Shanklin	W18	Bonchurch
W15	Ventnor		

All were withdrawn between 1923 and 1933. The original 'Ryde' was retained at Eastleigh for a number of years with a view to preservation, but unfortunately this never materialised.

There was also a 0-6-0ST named 'Bembridge': this engine was disposed of in 1917.

Isle of Wight Central Railway

This railway did not name its locomotives, but after absorption by the S.R. in 1923 three of the survivors were given names in accordance with the policy of naming all engines in the island.

I.W.C. No.	S.R. No.	Name
10	W10	Cowes
11	W11	Newport
12	W12	Ventnor

These were all former L.B.S.C. Stroudley 'Terrier' 0-6-0T's, for further particulars of which reference may be found under that Company. Nos. 10 and 12 were withdrawn from service in 1936 and lay for a number of years at Eastleigh before being broken up. No. 11 eventually returned to service on the mainland and assumed its correct number 2640 (afterwards B.R. 32640) in the L.B.S.C. series, at the same time losing its name.

Freshwater, Yarmouth and Newport Railway

The third and smallest railway in the Isle of Wight possessed two locomotives only, unnamed in independent days, but named by the S.R. after the grouping.

F.Y.N.R. No.	S.R. No.	Name
1	W1	Medina
2	W2 later W8	Freshwater

No. 1 was a 0-6-0ST built by Manning Wardle in 1902 (actually the newest engine ever to run in the island!) and was withdrawn from service in 1932.

No. 2 was a former L.B. & S.C.R. 'Terrier', which eventually returned to the mainland and assumed its correct number in the B.R. list, 32646, and losing its name at the same time.

Southern Railway (Isle of Wight)

The original stock of the three independent railways in the Isle of Wight has been dealt with in the preceding pages, but there remain a number of other engines transferred to the island after the grouping and named accordingly. They included three of Stroudley's 'Terriers' class 0-6-0T's already found on two of the Isle of Wight systems, and four of the later E1 class of 0-6-0T.

The 'Terriers', or 'A-1-X's' were as follows:—

Number before transfer	Isle of Wight No.	Name
LBSC 677	W3 later W13	Carisbrooke
LBSC 678	W4 later W14	Bembridge
SR B650	W9	Fishbourne

'Bembridge' was scrapped in 1936, 'Carisbrooke' returned to the mainland as B.R. 32677, and 'Fishbourne' as 515 S in the Departmental list, both losing their names.

The E 1's were as follows:—

S.R. Nos.	Isle of Wight No.	Name
B136	W1	Medina
B152	W2	Yarmouth
B154	W3	Ryde
B131	W4	Wroxall

All were scrapped between 1956 and 1960.

The principal class of engine allocated by the S.R. for working in the Isle of Wight however consisted of a number of Mr Adam's 4' 10" 0-4-4T's, and particulars of these will be found in the section dealing with the L. & S.W.R. on page 108.

Southern Railway

In 1925, at which period the newly formed Southern Railway was not held in very high estimation in the minds of the users of the line, a vigorous policy of rejuvenation was embarked upon, including a certain amount of modernisation of its locomotive stock. As a sidelight on this it was decided in future to name all of its principal express locomotives, a policy not hitherto adopted by either the L.S.W.R. or S.E. & C.R., or latterly by the L.B. & S.C.R.

Besides applying names to some of the existing South Western and Brighton engines, details of which will be found under those respective railways, new construction embodied the following classes:—

MAUNSELL'S 'KING ARTHUR' CLASS 4-6-0's
(development of Urie's final class, see page 110).

Built 1925–1927. The names chosen, as were also those now applied to the original South Western engines, were all associated with the legends of King Arthur's Knights of the Round Table.

The names were applied by horizontal plates over the centre driving wheel.

448	Sir Tristram		455	Sir Lancelot
449	Sir Torre		456	Sir Galahad
450	Sir Kay		457	Sir Bedivere
451	Sir Lamorak		763	Sir Bors de Ganis
452	Sir Meliagrance		764	Sir Gawain
453	King Arthur		765	Sir Gareth
454	Queen Guinevere		766	Sir Geraint

767	Sir Valence*	787	Sir Menadeuke
768	Sir Balin	788	Sir Urre of the Mount*
769	Sir Balan	789	Sir Guy
770	Sir Prianius	790	Sir Villiars
771	Sir Sagramore	791	Sir Uwaine
772	Sir Percivale	792	Sir Hervis de Revel
773	Sir Lavaine	793	Sir Ontzlake
774	Sir Gaheris	794	Sir Ector de Maris
775	Sir Agravaine	795	Sir Dinadan
776	Sir Galagars	796	Sir Dodinas le Savage
777	Sir Lamiel	797	Sir Blamor de Ganis
778	Sir Pelleas	798	Sir Hectimere
779	Sir Colgrevance	799	Sir Ironside
780	Sir Persant	800	Sir Meleaus de Lile
781	Sir Aglovale	801	Sir Meliot de Logres
782	Sir Brian	802	Sir Durnore
783	Sir Gillemere	803	Sir Harry le Fise Lake
784	Sir Nerovens	804	Sir Cador of Cornwall
785	Sir Mador de la Porte	805	Sir Constantine
786	Sir Lionel	806	Sir Galleron

* No. 767 was to have been named 'Sir Modred', and No. 788 'Sir Beaumains', but these were changed before the engines appeared. It was realised in time that 'Sir Modred' was a traitor, and as such hardly a suitable person to be commemorated.

All of these engines became B.R. 30448–30457 and 30763–30806. Withdrawal took place between 1959 and 1962, but No. 777 has been retained for preservation.

MAUNSELL 4 CYLINDER 4-6-0's 'LORD NELSON' CLASS
BUILT 1926–1929

850	Lord Nelson	858	Lord Duncan
851	Sir Francis Drake	859	Lord Hood
852	Sir Walter Raleigh	860	Lord Hawke
853	Sir Richard Grenville	861	Lord Anson
854	Howard of Effingham	862	Lord Collingwood
855	Robert Blake	863	Lord Rodney
856	Lord St. Vincent	864	Sir Martin Frobisher
857	Lord Howe	865	Sir John Hawkins

All became B.R. 30850–30865, and were withdrawn in 1961 and 1962. No. 850 is scheduled for preservation.

MAUNSELL 3 CYLINDER 4-4-0's 'SCHOOLS' CLASS

These engines, undoubtedly amongst the most successful of 4-4-0 designs ever constructed, appeared between 1930 and 1934.

900	Eton	904	Lancing
901	Winchester	905	Tonbridge
902	Wellington	906	Sherborne
903	Charterhouse	907	Dulwich

908	Westminster	924	Haileybury
909	St. Paul's	925	Cheltenham
910	Merchant Taylors	926	Repton
911	Dover	927	Clifton
912	Downside	928	Stowe
913	Christ's Hospital	929	Malvern
914	Eastbourne	930	Radley
915	Brighton	931	Kings-Wimbledon
916	Whitgift	932	Blundells
917	Ardingly	933	Kings-Canterbury
918	Hurstpierpoint	934	St. Lawrence†
919	Harrow	935	Sevenoaks
920	Rugby	936	Cranleigh
921	Shrewsbury	937	Epsom
922	Marlborough	938	St. Olaves
923	Uppingham/Bradfield*	939	Leatherhead

* The name 'Uppingham' was carried only for a short time. It is believed that the school authorities for some obscure reason objected to the name appearing on a locomotive.

† Temporarily renamed 'Westminster' in 1938.

These engines duly became B.R. Nos. 30900–30939 and withdrawal took place in 1961/2. No. 925 is scheduled for official preservation.

No. 928 has been privately preserved, and it is also reported that No. 926 may go to the U.S.A.

MAUNSELL'S 2-6-4T's CLASS K

As mentioned on page 111 the original engine of this class was built for the S.E. & C.R., but it did not receive its name until it came into S.R. ownership, when nineteen more were constructed, the whole series then running as follows:—

A790	River Avon	A800	River Cray
A791	River Adur	A801	River Darenth
A792	River Arun	A802	River Chuckmere
A793	River Ouse	A803	River Itchen
A794	River Rother	A804	River Tamar
A795	River Medway	A805	River Camel
A796	River Stour	A806	River Torridge
A797	River Mole	A807	River Axe
A798	River Wey	A808	River Char
A799	River Test	A809	River Dart

After the disastrous Sevenoaks accident in 1927 all of them were converted to 2-6-0 tender engines and lost their names in the process. This was not the first occasion on which the association of rivers with engine names seems to have produced unlucky results, as the instance of the Highland Railway engines mentioned on page 70 is another case in point. All of these engines duly became Nos. 1790–1809 and B.R. 31790–31809.

A further twenty engines were on order at the time of the accident, which were to have been named as under:—

A610	River Beaulieu	A620	River Lymington
A611	River Blackwater	A621	River Medina
A612	River Bowen	A622	River Meon
A613	River Bray	A623	River Okement
A614	River Creedy	A624	River Otter
A615	River Ebble	A625	River Parrett
A616	River Eden	A626	River Sid
A617	River Anton	A627	River Tavy
A618	River Hamble	A628	River Thames
A619	River Wandle	A629	River Titchfield

In the event, they were constructed new as 2-6-0 tender engines and never bore their allotted names.

MAUNSELL 2-6-4T CLASS K1

A 3 cylinder version of class K, of which only one was built, No. A890 'River Frome'.

Its subsequent history exactly followed the lines of the 2 cylinder engines.

BULLEID 'MERCHANT NAVY' PACIFICS

These remarkable engines were introduced during the war years, the first ten appearing during 1941/2. Ten more followed in 1944/5 and a further ten after Nationalisation in 1948. Under S.R. auspices the first twenty received the numbers 21C1 to 21C20, under a somewhat curious number scheme introduced by Mr Bulleid, but under Nationalisation they received more rational numbers 35001–35020, whilst the last twenty were turned out new as 35021–35030. All were built with streamlined casing which has now been removed. The complete list is as follows:—

35001	Channel Packet	35016	Elders Fyffes
35002	Union Castle	35017	Belgian Marine
35003	Royal Mail	35018	British India Line
35004	Cunard White Star	35019	French Line CGT
35005	Canadian Pacific	35020	Bibby Line
35006	Peninsular & Orient S.N. Co.	35021	New Zealand Line
35007	Aberdeen Commonwealth	35022	Holland-America Line
35008	Orient Line	35023	Holland-Afrika Line
35009	Shaw Savill	35024	East Asiatic Company
35010	Blue Star	35025	Brocklebank Line
35011	General Steam Navigation	35026	Lamport & Holt Line
35012	United States Line	35027	Port Line
35013	Blue Funnel	35028	Clan Line
35014	Nederland Line	35029	Ellerman Lines
35015	Rotterdam Lloyd	35030	Elder Dempster Lines

BULLEID 'WEST COUNTRY' PACIFICS

A slightly lighter version of the previous class. Like the 'Merchant Navies', the first seventy, which were built in 1945–1947, appeared as Nos. 21C101–21C170, but the final forty, built in 1948–1950, came out as 34071–34110, whereafter the original lot were renumbered 34001–34070.

The first forty eight of these engines were given names associated with the West Country, and this also applied to some of the later ones, but from 34049 onwards the majority were given names in commemoration of the Battle of Britain, and these particular engines are designated 'Battle of Britain' class, although there is no actual difference between them and the 'West Countries'. Most of the names are of Air Force Squadrons, but a few personalities also are included, outstanding of which shines 34051 'Winston Churchill'. This is very fittingly the engine of the class scheduled for preservation.

Like the 'Merchant Navies', these engines were built with streamlined casing, but this has since been removed from half of the class, the other retaining the 'air smoothing' as it is sometimes called, and it now seems unlikely that these will be similarly modified.

34001	Exeter	34030	Watersmeet
34002	Salisbury	34031	Torrington
34003	Plymouth	34032	Camelford
34004	Yeovil	34033	Chard
34005	Barnstaple	34034	Honiton
34006	Bude	34035	Shaftesbury
34007	Wadebridge	34036	Westward Ho
34008	Padstow	34037	Clovelly
34009	Lyme Regis	34038	Lynton
34010	Sidmouth	34039	Boscastle
34011	Tavistock	34040	Crewkerne
34012	Launceston	34041	Wilton
34013	Okehampton	34042	Dorchester
34014	Budleigh Salterton	34043	Combe Martin
34015	Exmouth	34044	Woolacombe
34016	Bodmin	34045	Ottery St. Mary
34017	Ilfracombe	34046	Braunton
34018	Axminster	34047	Callington
34019	Bideford	34048	Crediton
34020	Seaton	34049	Anti-Aircraft Command
34021	Dartmoor	34050	Royal Observer Corps
34022	Exmoor	34051	Winston Churchill
34023	Blackmore Vale	34052	Lord Dowding
34024	Tamar Valley	34053	Sir Keith Park
34025	Whimple	34054	Lord Beaverbrook
34026	Yes Tor	34055	Fighter Pilot
34027	Taw Valley	34056	Croydon
34028	Eddystone	34057	Biggin Hill
34029	Lundy	34058	Sir Frederick Pile

Great Southern Railway 4-6-0 No. 800, showing the nameplate 'Maeve' in Irish lettering.

Great Southern and Western Railway 0-4-2T 'Sprite'.

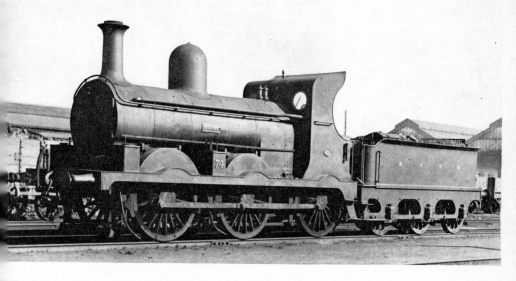

dland Great Western Railway No. 74 'Luna' in 1929 the last engine to lose its name consequent on absorption into the G.S.R.

Schull and Skibbereen 4-4-0T 'Kent', the peculiar formation of the letter 'K' will be noted.

Great Northern Railway of Ireland 4-4-0 'Neptune'.

G.N.R. (I) type of nameplate as used in more recent years.

G.N.R. (I) 4-4-0 No. 207, another case of necessary substitution of the original cast plate by a wooden replica

Dundalk Newry and Greenore Railway, an Irish offshoot of the L.N.W.R. These engines were of pure Crewe design, even down to the number-plates, but the name-plates were of a type not found on the parent company.

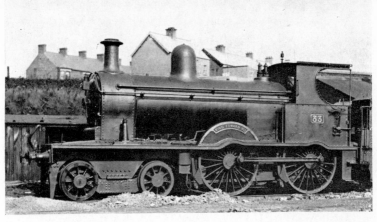

M.R. (N.C.C.) former Belfast and Northern Counties 4-4-0 'King Edward VII'.

[*R. M. Casserley*

A more recent L.M.S.R. (N.C.C.) 2-6-0 'Thomas Somerset'.

Sligo Leitrim and Northern Counties Railway 'Lissadell'. The engines of this railway never bore numbers.

County Donegal Railways Joint Committee No. 9.

Kent and East Sussex Railway 2-4-0T No. 1.

Shropshire and Montgomery Railway—0-4-2T 'Gazelle' now preserved by the W.D. at Longmoor.

Shropshire and Montgomery Railway—0-4-2ST 'Severn'.

34059	Sir Archibald Sinclair	34086	219 Squadron
34060	25 Squadron	34087	145 Squadron
34061	73 Squadron	34088	213 Squadron
34062	17 Squadron	34089	602 Squadron
34063	229 Squadron	34090	Sir Eustace Missenden,
34064	Fighter Command		Southern Railway
34065	Hurricane	34091	Weymouth
34066	Spitfire	34092	Wells/City of Wells
34067	Tangmere	34093	Saunton
34068	Kenley	34094	Mortehoe
34069	Hawkinge	34095	Brentor
34070	Manston	34096	Trevone
34071	601 Squadron	34097	Holsworthy
34072	257 Squadron	34098	Templecombe
34073	249 Squadron	34099	Lynmouth
34074	46 Squadron	34100	Appledore
34075	264 Squadron	34101	Hartland
34076	41 Squadron	34102	Lapford
34077	603 Squadron	34103	Calstock
34078	222 Squadron	34104	Bere Alston
34079	141 Squadron	34105	Swanage
34080	74 Squadron	34106	Lydford
34081	92 Squadron	34107	Blandford Forum
34082	615 Squadron	34108	Wincanton
34083	605 Squadron	34109	Sir Trafford Leigh-Mallory
34084	253 Squadron	34110	66 Squadron
34085	501 Squadron		

No. 34051, 'Winston Churchill' which had the honour of conveying the great man's mortal remains to his last resting place, is being preserved.

Other Southern Railway engines which remain to be mentioned, include a Barclay 0-4-0ST 'The Master General' built in 1910, which became S.R. property in 1928 when purchased from the Mersey Docks & Harbour Board. It spent its time on the S.R. at Southampton Docks, but was allocated no number in that Company's list. It was withdrawn in 1945.

Then there was a 0-8-0T purchased in 1932 from the Kent & East Sussex Railway (see page 161), No. 4 'Hecate', which became S.R. 949. Scrapped 1950.

U.S.A. 0-6-0T's

Two of the 14 of these engines purchased by the S.R. in 1947 were transferred to the Departmental list for shunting at Ashford works in 1963, and both were named after former S.E. & C.R. locomotive superintendents.

Original S.R.	*B.R.*	*Departmental No.*	*Name*
65	30065	D.S. 237	Maunsell
70	30070	D.S. 238	Wainwright

Both were still active towards the close of 1966.

K

V
British Railways Designs

BRITISH RAILWAYS 'BRITANNIA' CLASS PACIFIC

Introduced 1951

70000	Britannia	70028	Royal Star
70001	Lord Hurcomb	70029	Shooting Star
70002	Geoffrey Chaucer	70030	William Wordsworth
70003	John Bunyan	70031	Byron
70004	William Shakespeare	70032	Tennyson
70005	John Milton	70033	Charles Dickens
70006	Robert Burns	70034	Thomas Hardy
70007	Coeur-de-Lion	70035	Rudyard Kipling
70008	Black Prince	70036	Boadicea
70009	Alfred the Great	70037	Hereward the Wake
70010	Owen Glendower	70038	Robin Hood
70011	Hotspur	70039	Sir Christopher Wren
70012	John of Gaunt	70040	Clive of India
70013	Oliver Cromwell	70041	Sir John Moore
70014	Iron Duke	70042	Lord Roberts
70015	Apollo	70043	Lord Kitchener
70016	Ariel	70044	Earl Haigh
70017	Arrow	70045	Lord Rowallan
70018	Flying Dutchman	70046	Anzac
70019	Lightning	70048	The Territorial Army,
70020	Mercury		1908–1958
70021	Morning Star	70049	Solway Firth
70022	Tornado	70050	Firth of Clyde
70023	Venus	70051	Firth of Forth
70024	Vulcan	70052	Firth of Tay
70025	Western Star	70053	Moray Firth
70026	Polar Star	70054	Dornoch Firth
70027	Rising Star		

It will be noticed that one number, 70047, is missing from this list. For some unknown reason this locomotive has never been allocated a name.

BRITISH RAILWAYS 'CAPROTTI' PACIFIC

Built in 1954, this was intended to be the prototype of a new heavy duty express passenger type, but unfortunately owing to the decision to con-

130

centrate on diesel construction, it was destined to remain the only one of its class, and after a short life of only eight years, was withdrawn in 1962.

71000   Duke of Gloucester

BRITISH RAILWAYS 'CLAN' CLASS PACIFIC

Introduced 1952 for lighter express passenger duties.

72000	Clan Buchanan	72005	Clan Macgregor
72001	Clan Cameron	72006	Clan Mackenzie
72003	Clan Campbell	72007	Clan Mackintosh
72004	Clan Fraser	72008	Clan Macleod
72005	Clan Macdonald	72009	Clan Stewart

A further fifteen were to have been constructed in 1955, but unfortunately the order was cancelled and the engines were never built. As a matter of interest, their allocated numbers and names are given:—

72010	Hengist	72018	Clan Maclean
72011	Horsa	72019	Clan Douglas
72012	Canute	72020	Clan Gordon
72013	Wildfire	72021	Clan Hamilton
72014	Firebrand	72022	Clan Kennedy
72015	Clan Colquhoun	72023	Clan Lindsay
72016	Clan Graham	72024	Clan Scott
72017	Clan MacDougall		

BRITISH RAILWAYS CLASS 5 MIXED TRAFFIC 4-6-0's

Introduced 1951. Twenty of these engines attached to the Southern Region have been given names, reviving those formerly carried by the original Urie 'King Arthurs' Nos. 30736–30755 (see page 110).

73080	Merlin	73110	The Red Knight
73081	Excalibur	73111	King Uther
73082	Camelot	73112	Morgan le Fay
73083	Pendragon	73113	Lyonesse
73084	Tintagel	73114	Etarre
73085	Melisande	73115	King Pellinore
73086	The Green Knight	73116	Iseult
73087	Linette	73117	Vivien
73088	Joyous Gard	73118	King Leodegrance
73089	Maid of Astolat	73119	Elaine

BRITISH RAILWAYS 'AUSTERITY' 2-8-0's

Seven hundred and thirty-three of these engines built during the war years were eventually acquired by B.R. The last of them, No. 90732, was given the name 'Vulcan', carried on a plate on the cabside. It was originally built by the Vulcan Foundry as War Department No. 79312. It was scrapped in 1962.

BRITISH RAILWAYS 'AUSTERITY' 2-10-0's

Twenty-five of these engines built by the North British Loco Company in 1945 came into the hands of B.R. as Nos. 90750–90774 and somewhat oddly, both of the last two, Nos. 90773 and 90774, carried the name 'North British' on plates affixed to the sides of the boiler barrel. It has since been removed from both engines. They were originally War Department Nos. 73798 and 73799.

BRITISH RAILWAYS STANDARD CLASS 9 2-10-0's

No. 92220 of this class, turned out by Swindon works in March 1960, was the last new steam locomotive to be built for British Railways. It was appropriately named 'Evening Star' with handsome nameplates in true Great Western style attached to the smoke deflectors.

WESTERN REGION DIESEL HYDRAULIC 'WARSHIP' CLASS, INTRODUCED 1958

The nameplates on these engines are cast in the old G.W.R. style with its handsome type of lettering, and are of distinctive appearance.

D600	Active	D818	Glory
D601	Ark Royal	D819	Goliath
D602	Bulldog	D820	Grenville
D603	Conquest	D821	Greyhound
D604	Cossack	D822	Hercules
D800	Sir Brian Robertson	D823	Hermes
D801	Vanguard	D824	Highflyer
D802	Formidable	D825	Intrepid
D803	Albion	D826	Jupiter
D804	Avenger	D827	Kelly
D805	Benbow	D828	Magnificent
D806	Cambrian	D829	Magpie
D807	Caradoc	D830	Majestic
D808	Centuar	D831	Monarch
D809	Champion	D832	Onslaught
D810	Cockade	D833	Panther
D811	Daring	D834	Pathfinder
D812	Royal Naval Reserve 1859–1959	D835	Pegasus
		D836	Powerful
D813	Diadem	D837	Ramillies
D814	Dragon	D838	Rapid
D815	Druid	D839	Relentless
D816	Eclipse	D840	Resistance
D817	Foxhound	D841	Roebuck

D842	Royal Oak	D857	Undaunted
D843	Sharpshooter	D858	Valorous
D844	Spartan	D859	Vanquisher
D845	Sprightly	D860	Victorious
D846	Steadfast	D861	Vigilant
D847	Strongbow	D862	Viking
D848	Sultan	D863	Warrior
D849	Superb	D864	Zambesi
D850	Swift	D865	Zealous
D851	Temeraire	D866	Zebra
D852	Tenacious	D867	Zenith
D853	Thruster	D868	Zephyr
D854	Tiger	D869	Zest
D855	Triumph	D870	Zulu
D856	Trojan		

WESTERN REGION DIESEL HYDRAULIC 'WESTERN' CLASS, INTRODUCED 1961

These nameplates are of plainer pattern than those on the 'Warships', but the names themselves at any rate follow Western tradition to a somewhat extraordinary degree:—

D1000	Western Enterprise		D1026	Western Centurion	
D1001	„	Pathfinder	D1027	„	Lancer
D1002	„	Explorer	D1028	„	Hussar
D1003	„	Pioneer	D1029	„	Legionaire
D1004	„	Crusader	D1030	„	Musketeer
D1005	„	Venturer	D1031	„	Rifleman
D1006	„	Stalwart	D1032	„	Marksman
D1007	„	Talisman	D1033	„	Trooper
D1008	„	Harrier	D1034	„	Dragoon
D1009	„	Invader	D1035	„	Yeoman
D1010	„	Campaigner	D1036	„	Emperor
D1011	„	Thunderer	D1037	„	Empress
D1012	„	Firebrand	D1038	„	Sovereign
D1013	„	Ranger	D1039	„	King
D1014	„	Leviathan	D1040	„	Queen
D1015	„	Champion	D1041	„	Prince
D1016	„	Gladiator	D1042	„	Princess
D1017	„	Warrior	D1043	„	Duke
D1018	„	Buccaneer	D1044	„	Duchess
D1019	„	Challenger	D1045	„	Viscount
D1020	„	Hero	D1046	„	Marquis
D1021	„	Cavalier	D1047	„	Lord
D1022	„	Sentinel	D1048	„	Lady
D1023	„	Fusilier	D1049	„	Monarch
D1024	„	Huntsman	D1050	„	Ruler
D1025	„	Guardsman	D1051	„	Ambassador

D1052	Western Viceroy		D1063	Western Monitor
D1053	„	Patriarch	D1064	„	Regent
D1054	„	Governor	D1065	„	Consort
D1055	„	Advocate	D1066	„	Prefect
D1056	„	Sultan	D1067	„	Druid
D1057	„	Chieftain	D1068	„	Reliance
D1058	„	Nobleman	D1069	„	Vanguard
D1059	„	Empire	D1070	„	Gauntlet
D1060	„	Dominion	D1071	„	Renown
D1061	„	Envoy	D1072	„	Glory
D1062	„	Courier	D1073	„	Bulwark

ENGLISH ELECTRIC 'DELTIC' CLASS INTRODUCED 1961

D9000	Royal Scots Grey	D9011	The Royal Northumberland Fusiliers
D9001	St. Paddy		
D9002	The King's Own Yorkshire Light Infantry	D9012	Crepello
		D9013	The Black Watch
D9003	Meld	D9014	The Duke of Wellington's Regiment
D9004	Queen's Own Highlander		
D9005	The Prince of Wales's Own Regiment of Yorkshire	D9015	Tulyar
		D9016	Gordon Highlander
		D9017	The Durham Light Infantry
D9006	The Fife and Forfar Yeomanry	D9018	Ballymoss
		D9019	Royal Highland Fusilier
D9007	Pinza	D9020	Nimbus
D9008	The Green Howards	D9021	Argyll and Sutherland Highlander
D9009	Alycidon		
D9010	The King's Own Scottish Borderer		

BRITISH RAILWAYS DIESEL LOCOMOTIVES

Sulzer 'Peak' class, introduced 1959. Only a few of these engines carry names:—

D1	Scafell Pike	D52	The Lancashire Fusilier
D2	Helvellyn	D53	Royal Tank Regiment
D3	Skiddaw	D54	The Royal Pioneer Corps
D4	Great Gable	D55	Royal Signals
D5	Cross Fell	D56	The Bedfordshire & Hertfordshire Regiment (T.A.)
D6	Whernside		
D7	Ingleborough		
D8	Penyghent	D58	The King's Own Royal Border Regiment
D9	Snowdon		
D10	Tryfan	D59	The Royal Warwickshire Fusilier
D49	The Manchester Regiment		
D50	King's Shropshire Light Infantry	D60	Lytham St. Annes
		D61	Royal Army Ordnance Corps

D62	5th Royal Inniskilling	D77	Royal Irish Fusilier
	Dragoon Guards	D84	Royal Corps of Transport
D63	Royal Inniskilling Fusilier	D89	Honourable Artillery
D64	Coldstream Guardsman		Company
D65	Grenadier Guardsman	D99	3rd Carabinier
D67	Royal Artilleryman	D100	Sherwood Forester
D70	Royal Marines	D137	The Cheshire Regiment
D71	The Staffordshire Regiment	D163	Leicestershire & Derbyshire
	(The Prince of Wales's)		Yeomanry

ENGLISH ELECTRIC 2000 HP TYPE 4

Introduced 1958. Some of the earlier engines of this series have now received names, in the form of a small and somewhat insignificant rectangular plate on the side of the locomotive.

D210	Empress of Britain	D223	Lancastria
D211	Mauretania	D224	Lucania
D212	Aureol	D225	Lusitania
D213	Andania	D227	Parthia
D214	Antonia	D228	Samaria
D215	Aquitania	D229	Saxonia
D216	Campania	D230	Scythia
D217	Carinthia	D231	Sylvania
D218	Carmania	D232	Empress of Canada
D219	Caronia	D233	Empress of England
D220	Franconia	D234	Accra
D221	Ivernia	D235	Apapa
D222	Laconia		

BRUSH 2750 H.P. TYPE 4, INTRODUCED 1962

Built in considerable numbers, but only a few allocated to the Western Region bear names.

D1660	City of Truro	D1666	Odin
D1661	North Star	D1671	Thor*
D1662	Isambard Kingdom Brunel	D1672	Colossus
D1663	Sir Daniel Gooch	D1674	Samson
D1664	George Jackson	D1677	Thor
	Churchward		

* This engine was scrapped in 1966 after being involved in an accident, and the nameplates transferred to D 1677.

ELECTRIC LOCOMOTIVES

L.N.E.R. and B.R. (EASTERN REGION)

Only the first of these locomotives was actually built by the L.N.E.R., the remainder followed in the 1950's under Nationalisation.

The original engine, turned out as No. 6701 in 1941, was the pioneer of the class for working the Manchester and Sheffield electrification, on which work was suspended until after the war. It became No. 6000 under the 1946 re-numbering scheme and eventually was named, along with certain others of the subsequent engines, as follows:—

26000	Tommy	26052	Nestor
26046	Archimedes	26053	Perseus
26047	Diomedes	26054	Pluto
26048	Hector	26055	Prometheus
26049	Jason	26056	Triton
26050	Stentor	26057	Ulysses
26051	Mentor		

The above were mixed traffic engines capable of working both passenger and freight trains. A further series of express passenger engines appeared in 1954.

27000	Electra	27004	Juno
27001	Ariadne	27005	Minerva
27002	Aurora	27006	Pandora
27003	Diana		

VI
Irish Railways

Great Southern and Western Railway

The largest railway in Ireland, the G.S. & W.R. did not normally name its locomotives, although there are a few exceptions, mainly small tank engines which were given names in lieu of numbers—it apparently being considered unnecessary that they should carry both.

Four 4-4-0 express locomotives turned out at Inchicore in 1900, however, bore names for a time, although these were subsequently removed.

301	Victoria	303	St. Patrick
302	Lord Roberts	304	Princess Ena

Another large 4-4-0, built by Mr Maunsell in 1913 (before he departed for the South Eastern and Chatham) was No. 341 'Sir William Goulding'. This engine had a particularly short life, especially for Irish locomotives, and was withdrawn in 1928.

The Irish grouping, embracing all lines which came entirely within the boundaries of what had then become the Irish Free State, took place in 1925, when the G.S. & W.R. absorbed the remaining companies and became the Great Southern Railway. This again was taken over by the State in 1945, and was thereafter known as Coras Iompair Eireann (Transport Company of Ireland). Of Nos. 301–304 mentioned above, all had been rebuilt and modernised and lasted until comparatively recently, the last three until 1957–1959, whilst No. 301 was still in existence in 1962.

The only other main line engines with names were three large 4-6-0's built at Inchicore in 1939, and which were in fact the last new steam engines to be constructed for the C.I.E.

800	Maeve	801	Macha	802	Tailte

They were named after former Queens of Ireland, with handsome nameplates in Irish lettering over the centre driving wheels. Consequent on the total dieselisation of the C.I.E., which was completed in 1964, they latterly became redundant, No. 802 being scrapped in 1957 and 801 in 1962. No. 800 is preserved in Belfast Museum.

The miscellaneous unnumbered tank engines were as follows:—

| Sambo | 0-4-2ST | Built 1914 | Shunter at Inchicore still in existence in 1962 but with name removed. |

Sprite	0-4-2T	„	1873	Scrapped about 1933
Fairy	„	„	1894	„ 1927
Negro	0-6-4T	„	1876	„ 1910
Jumbo	0-6-0T (originally 0-6-4T)	„	„	„ 1957

The G.S. & W.R. absorbed previously the independent Waterford Limerick and Western Railway about the turn of the century, and in renumbering the loco stock into its own list proceeded to remove the names which these engines had carried in the process. Other miscellaneous acquisitions about this time were a couple of 0-6-0ST's, 'Shamrock', from the Fenit Harbour Commissioners, which became G.S. & W.R. No. 299, and 'Erin' from the Waterford and Wexford Railway, which although allocated the number 300, for some reason never actually carried it.

The Waterford and Wexford also had a 0-4-0T named 'Cambria'. This was not given a number in the G.S. & W.R. list and was sold to the Dublin and Blessington Tramway in 1918.

The principal railways absorbed at the 1925 amalgamation were the Midland Great Western and the Dublin & South Eastern, both of which named most of its locomotives. There were in addition a number of small lines mostly of narrow gauge, but there was also the standard (5' 3") gauge Timoleague and Courtmacsherry Railway, possessing two locomotives, and these, with true Irish inconsistency, were left with their names and not renumbered into the standard gauge stock.

St. Molaga	0-4-2T	Built 1890	Scrapped 1949
Argadeen	2-6-0T	„ 1894	„ about 1957

The narrow gauge lines, too, were not all treated alike, as whilst some of them which had named engines lost them rapidly, in other cases they were retained for a number of years. The locos from these lines were not renumbered into the general list.

Cork and Muskerry Railway

1	City of Cork	4-4-0T	Built 1887	Scrapped	1935
2	Coachford	„	„ „	„	„
3	St. Annes	„	„ „	„	1924
4	Blarney	0-4-2WT	„ 1888	„	1911
4	Blarney	4-4-0T	„ 1919	„	1927
5	Donoughmore	0-4-4T	„ 1892	„	1937

6	The Muskerry	0-4-4T	Built 1893	Scrapped	1954*
7	Peake	4-4-0T	„ 1898	„	1935
8	Dripsey	„	„ 1904	„	1935

* Transferred in 1938 to the Schull and Skibbereen
All lost their names at the amalgamation.

Schull and Skibbereen Railway

1	Marion	0-4-0T tram	Built 1886	Scrapped	1906
1	Gabriel	4-4-0T	„ 1906	„	1936
2	Ida	0-4-0T tram	„ 1886	„	1926
3	Ilen	„ „	„ „	„	1914
3	Kent	4-4-0T	„ 1914	„	1954
4	Erin	„	„ 1888	„	1954

'Kent' may have retained its name to the end, but 'Erin' had lost hers.

West and South Clare Railway

1	Kilrush	4-6-0T	Built 1912	Scrapped	1953
2	Ennis	2-6-2T	„ 1900	„	1955
3	Ennistymon	4-6-0T	„ 1922	„	1953
4	Liscannor	2-6-2T	„ 1901	„	1928
5	Slieve Callan	0-6-2T	„ 1892	Withdrawn	1960*
6	Saint Senan	„	„ „	Scrapped	1956
7	Lady Inchiquin	„	„ „	„	1922
7	Malbay	4-6-0T	„ 1922	„	1954
8	Lisdoonvarna	2-6-2T	„ 1894	„	1925
9	Fergus	„	„ 1898	„	1954
10	Lahinch	4-6-0T	„ 1903	„	1953
11	Kilkee	„	„ 1909	„	1953

* Preserved at Ennis
All had lost their names.

Cavan and Leitrim Railway

1	Isabel	4-4-0T	Built 1884	Scrapped	1949
2	Kathleen	„	„ „	Withdrawn	1959*
3	Lady Edith	„	„ „	„	1959*
4	Violet	„	„ „	Scrapped	1960
5	Gertrude	„	„ „	„	1925
6	May	„	„ „	„	1927
7	Olive	„	„ „	„	1945
8	Queen Victoria	„	„ „	„	1959
9	King Edward	0-6-4T	„ 1904	„	1934

* No. 2 is preserved in Belfast Museum and No. 3 was sent to the U.S.A. Nos. 1, 2, 4, 7, and 9 retained their names for many years after amalgamation, in most cases until withdrawal.

Midland Great Western Railway

This was the second largest of the constituent Companies which were amalgamated in 1925 to form the Great Southern Railway, and at that time it possessed the distinction of having named the whole of its locomotive stock, with the exception of a few freight engines built towards the end of its existence. The names were carried in most cases on a plate on the side of the boiler barrel. The engines were renumbered in a separate series in the former G.S. & W.R. list between 530 and 668 and all de-named.

The oldest passenger engines at the time of the amalgamation were a series of 2-4-0's which had been built between 1893 and 1898.

G.S.R. No.	*Former M.G.W.R. No. and name*		*G.S.R. No.*	*Former M.G.W.R. No. and name*	
650	14	Racer	660	15	Rover
651	16	Rob Roy	661	17	Reindeer
652	18	Ranger	662	21	Swift
653	19	Spencer	663	22	Samson
654	28	Clara	664	23	Sylph
655	29	Clonsilla	665	24	Sprite
656	30	Active	666	27	Clifden
657	33	Arrow	667	31	Alert
658	34	Aurora	668	32	Ariel
659	13	Rapid			

All lasted until the 1950's and one or two were still at work in 1961, the last 2-4-0's to remain in service in the British Isles and possibly the whole world.

There had also been an earlier series of 2-4-0's built between 1883-7 and withdrawn 1915-1923.

1	Orion	41	Regal
4	Venus	42	Ouzel
5	Mars	43	Leinster
6	Vesta	44	Ulster
35	Airedale	45	Queen
36	Eagle	46	Munster
39	Hawk	47	Viceroy
40	Lily	48	Connaught

Most of the main line work was in the hands of 4-4-0's of various classes, some of which had been rebuilt from old 2-4-0's of 1880, and even the most recent of them dated back to 1915.

530	36/1	Empress of Austria	536	12	Shamrock
531	25/4	Cyclops	537	9/20	Emerald Isle
532	26/5	Britannia	538	4/25	Ballynahinch
533	37/6	Wolfdog	539	11/26	Croagh Patrick
534	2	Jupiter	540	7	Connemara
535	3	Juno	541	8	St. Patrick

542	6/9	Kylemore	547	125	Britannic
543	10	Faugh-a-Ballagh	548	126	Atlantic
544	11	Erin-go-Bragh	549	128	Majestic
545	127	Titanic	550	124	Mercuric
546	129	Celtic			

One or two of these were withdrawn in the 1930's, but most survived the second world war, one or two as late as 1959.

Various types of 0-6-0 were the maids-of-all-work for general service, having been built at various periods between 1876 and 1924. They may be summarised as under:—

233*	141	Limerick	596	57	Lough Corrib
234*	142	Athenry	597	58	Lough Gill
563	49	Marquis	598	59	Shannon
564	50	Viscount	599	60	Lough Owel
565	51	Baron	600	61	Lynx
566	52	Regent	601	62	Tiger
567	53	Duke	602	63	Lion
568	54	Earl	—	64	Leopard†
569	76	Lightning	603	65	Wolf
570	78	Planet	604	66	Elephant
571	83	Lucan	605	67	Dublin
572	84	Dunkellen	606	68	Mullingar
573	95/85	Bulldog	607	69	Athlone
574	80	Dunsandle	608	70	Ballinasloe
575	92/135	Bittern	609	71	Galway
576	74	Luna	610	72	Sligo
577	86	Bullfinch	611	140	Wren
578	79	Mayo	612	75	Hector
579	91/64	Bear	613	81	Clancarty
582	73	Comet	—	85	Meath†
583	82	Clonbrock	—	87	Buzzard†
584	130	Ajax	—	88	Buffalo†
585	131	Atlas	—	89	Bison†
586	132	Pluto	—	90	Beaver†
587	133	Titan	—	93	Butterfly†
588	134	Vulcan	—	94	Badger†
—	135	Arran Isles†	619	96	Avonside
589	77	Star	620	97	Hibernia
590	136	Cavan	621	98	Caledonia
591	137	Maynooth	622	99	Cambria
592	138	Nephin	646	143	Canada
593	139	Tara	647	144	Australia
594	55	Inny	648	145	India
595	56	Liffey	649	146	Africa

* Were to have become 580 and 581, but renumbered in lieu as shown.

† Scrapped by 1925 and not included in renumbering.

A few of the earlier engines did not survive long enough to carry their G.S.R. allocated numbers. No 74, 'Luna', was the last engine to remain in M.G.W.R. colours, and did not become G.S.R. 576 until 1931. A few of these 0-6-0's were still at work in 1962.

The M.G.W.R. had very few tank engines, made up entirely of two classes of 0-6-0T's. The smaller of these, which were actually of later construction, having been built in 1891-4, were as follows:—

551	106	Lark	557	112	Hornet
552	107	Robin	558	113	Gnat
553	108	Swallow	559	114	Stork
554	109	Fly	560	115	Achill
555	110	Bat	561	116	Cong
556	111	Wasp	562	117	Moy

No. 560 and possibly one or two others, was still active in 1961.

The larger 0-6-0T's, dating from 1881 to 1890, were as follows:—

614	100	Giantess
615	101	Giant
616	102	Pilot
617	103	Pioneer
618	105	Hercules

These engines disappeared in the 1950's.

Dublin and South Eastern Railway

Like the M.G.W.R., this Company's engines were absorbed into G.S.R. stock at the 1925 grouping. Most had already lost their names by 1925.

The main line traffic between Dublin and Rosslare was in the hands of five 4-4-0's, built in 1895 and 1905.

G.S.R. No.	Former D.S.E.R. No.	Name
450	55	Rathdown
451	56	Rathmines
452	57	Rathnew
453	58	Rathdrum
454	67	Rathmore
—	68	Rathcoole*

* Scrapped 1925 and not included in G.S.R. stock. The others went in the 1930's and 1940's.

There were some 2-4-0's dating from the 1860's, only one of which survived to be absorbed into G.S.R. stock.

G.S.R. No.	Former D.S.E.R. No.	Name	Scrapped
422	24	Glenmore	1928
—	25	Glenart	1925
—	31	Glen of the Downs	1923
—	32	Glenmalure	1925
—	33	Glendalough	1925

There had also been four 0-4-2 tender engines, none of which survived the amalgamation.

15 Barrow
37 Slaney
38 Nore
39 Suir

The D.S.E.R. had a small, but for Ireland, busy local service between Dublin and Bray, this was worked by 2-4-0's, 0-4-2T's, 2-4-2T's and 4-4-2T's.

The 2-4-0T's, mostly dating from the 1890's, were as follows:—

423	49	Carrickmines	—	26	Blackrock
424	9	Dalkey	—	41	Delgany
425	47	Stillorgan	—	42	Ballybrack
426	44	Dunleary	—	43	Shangannagh
—	2	Glenageary			

The last six were scrapped between 1923 and 1927, but Nos. 423–425 lasted until 1953-1955.

Also two small 0-4-2T's, which did not last into G.S.R. days:—

16 Killiney
21 Kilcoole
Both were scrapped in 1925.

The 2-4-2T's, most of which were rebuilds from 2-4-0T's, built between 1888 and 1909 (except for No. 427, which was an older engine originally belonging to the London and North Western Railway and altered to the Irish gauge) were:—

427	64	Earl of Bessborough	434	8	St. Brendan
428	3	St. Patrick	435	12	St. Brigid
429	10	St. Senanus	436	27	St. Aiden/ St. Aidan
430	11	St. Kevin			
431	28	St. Laurence	437	29	St. Mantan
432	45	St. Kieran	438	30	St. Iberius
433	46	Princess Mary	439	40	St. Selskar

In addition to No. 427, there had also been five other L.N.W.R. Webb 2-4-2T's, but these were returned to England in 1916/17.

59	Earl of Fitzwilliam	62	Earl of Meath
60	Earl of Courtown	63	Earl of Carysfort
61	Earl of Wicklow		

Nos. 60 and 62 were sold to the Government and worked at Richboro', Kent. After the war were again disposed of, to the Cramlington Colliery, Northumberland, where they lasted until about 1929.

The last survivors of these engines were scrapped in 1957.

The 4-4-2T's, built between 1893 and 1911, were:—

455	20	King George
458	52	Duke of Connaught
459	54	Duke of Abercorn
460	53	Duke of Leinster

The others, 456 and 457, were unnamed. Two of these engines lasted until 1960. For general purposes, there were ten 0-6-0's of varying designs, dated between 1897 and 1910.

440	17	Wicklow	445	65	Cork
441	36	Wexford	446	66	Dublin
442	13	Waterford	447	50	Arklow
443	14	Limerick	448	4	Lismore
444	18	Enniscorthy	449	5	Clonmel
			—	51	New Ross*

The last of these was scrapped in 1957.

* Scrapped 1925 without being renumbered.

Finally, there were two 0-4-0T's converted from rail motors, built in 1906, which for some reason were not given numbers in the G.S.R. stock.

D.S.E. No. 69 Elf   *D.S.E. No.* 70 Imp

These were scrapped in 1928 and 1931.

Great Northern Railway of Ireland

The G.N.R., the second largest Irish railway, ran partly in the Free State and partly in Northern Ireland, and was consequently unaffected by the 1925 grouping. Up to the time of the first world war it named most of its locomotives, the plates being usually affixed to the side of the boiler barrel, except with the later engines. These names were, however, all removed between 1912 and 1920, and, except in a few instances, never restored. It

Bishops Castle Railway
'Carlisle'.

Campbeltown & Machrihanish 0-6-2T 'Atlantic'.

Selsey Railway—'Ringing Rock'.

Ashover Light Railway 'Joan'.

Southwold Railway No. 3 'Blyth'.

[L.

Isle of Man Railway 2-4-0T No. 5 'Mona'.

Isle of Man Railway 0-6-0T No. 15, formerly
Manx Northern Railway.

Cannock Chase and Wolverhampton Railway, 'McClean', in 1946. It was then one of the oldest working locomotives in the country.

Eastwell Quarries, nameplate of French-built metre gauge engine.

Eastwell Quarries, 'The Baronet', built by the little known firm of Markham & Co. in 1889.

Furzebrook Railway 'Quintus', the fifth engine owned by the line.

Padarn Railway
'Cackler'.

Padarn Railway 'Fire Queen'. An
ancient 0-4-0 built in 1848 and
preserved at Llanberis.

Padarn Railway—
'Holy War'.

was not until 1958 that it was finally partitioned and the locomotive stock divided equally between the C.I.E. and the Ulster Transport Authority, the corresponding body in the north. Those transferred to the C.I.E. have retained their numbers, but the U.T.A. ones have been renumbered in that Company's lists.

4-2-2's

Two very handsome single wheelers, the only 4-2-2 express engines ever to run in Ireland, were built in 1885.

88 Victoria

89 Albert

They were rebuilt in 1904 as 4-4-0's and in common with all G.N.R. engines, lost their names at about the time of the first world war. Both were scrapped in 1956.

4-4-0's

The earlier 4-4-0's comprised several classes, built between 1885 and 1911, and may be summarised thus:—

12	Ulster	76	Hercules	123	Lucifer
15	Pansy	77	Achilles	124	Cerberus
24	Juno	82/27	Daisy	125	Daphne
25	Liffey	83/26	Narcissus	126	Diana
42	Munster	104	Ovoca	127	Erebus/
43	Lagan	105	Foyle		Hercules
44	Leinster	106	Tornado	128	Mars
45	Sirocco	107	Cyclone	129	Connaught
46	Typhoon	113	Neptune	130	Saturn
50	Donard	114	Theseus	131	Uranus
51	Hyacinth	115	Lily	132	Mercury
52	Snowdrop	116	Violet	133	Apollo
70	Precursor	117	Shamrock	134	Adonis
71	Bundoran	118	Rose	135	Cyclops
72	Daffodil	119	Thistle	136	Minerva
73	Primrose	120	Venus	156	Pandora
74	Rostrevor	121	Pluto	157	Orpheus
75	Jupiter	122	Vulcan		

Most of these had disappeared by 1959, but No. 132, transferred to the C.I.E., was still in service in 1962. Nos. 115–119, which were older engines, were withdrawn in the 1920's, but Nos. 118 and 119 went to the S.L. & N.C.R. (see page 152).

L

A larger class of 4-4-0's for the main line was introduced in 1913, followed by three more in 1915.

170	Errigal	173	Galtee More	191	Croagh Patrick
171	Slieve Gullion	174	Carrantuohill	192	Slievenamon
172	Slieve Donard	190	Lugnaquilla		

Nos. 170–174 lost their names about 1920, and Nos. 190–192 were not named at all when built. In 1939, however, the whole series was renewed and painted in a new livery of blue with scarlet underframes, the names of the first five being restored and new ones added to the last three. Most of them were still running in 1962, Nos. 172, 173, 190 and 192 having become U.T.A. Nos. 60–63. No. 171 has been acquired by the Irish Preservation Society.

An intermediate class of 4-4-0's were introduced in 1915 for cross country work, Nos. 196–200, then unnamed. From 1939 onwards these also were painted blue, and five others were constructed in 1947 to the same design.

196	Lough Gill	199	Lough Derg	202	Louth
197	Lough Neagh	200	Lough Melvin	203	Armagh
198	Lough Swilly	201	Meath	204	Antrim
				205	Down

On the division of stock Nos. 196, 200, 201, 202 and 205 became U.T.A. 64–68, the others remaining with the C.I.E., and most of the class were still running in 1962. (All scrapped by 1966.)

4-4-0 COMPOUNDS CLASS V

In 1932 came five large 4-cylinder compounds for working the accelerated Dublin–Belfast expresses, at first unnamed, but eventually as follows:—

83	Eagle	85	Merlin	87	Kestrel
84	Falcon	86	Peregrine		

The last survivor in 1962 was 'Merlin', now preserved.

4-4-0's CLASS VS

The last express engines, built in 1948, were five large 4-4-0's similar to the compounds, but with simple expansion:—

206	Liffey	208	Lagan	210	Erne
207	Boyne	209	Foyle		

Nos. 208 and 210 were running as U.T.A. 58 and 59 in 1962. No. 206 was scrapped in 1959. No. 207 was the last survivor.

0-6-0's

These comprised several classes, some dating from 1872 (Nos. 137 and 138, which were built for the Ulster Railway) to the most recent, turned out in 1915.

9	Kells	63	Donegal	140	Limerick
10	Bessbrook	64/67	Down	141	Westmeath
11	Dromore	65	Derry	142	Torrent
26	Armagh	66	Monaghan	143	Avalanche
27	Dublin	67/27/149	Fermanagh	144	Vesuvius
28	Wexford	68	Kildare	145	Carlow
29	Enniskillen	69	Newry	146	Wicklow
31	Galway	78/119	Pettigo	147	Hecla
32	Drogheda	79/69	Cavan	148	Teneriffe
33	Belfast	80	Antrim	149	Roscommon
34	Louth	81	Leitrim	150	Longford
35	Clare	100	Clones	151	Strabane
36	Waterford	101	Balmoral	152	Lurgan
38	Kesh	102	Belleek	153	Scarva
39	Beragh	103	Dunleer	154	Lambeg
55	Portadown	108	Pomeroy	155	Navan
56	Omagh	109	Moira	158	Ballybay
57	Cork	110	Laytown	159	Cootehill
58	Kerry	111	Malahide	160	Culloville
59	Kilkenny	112	Keady	161	Adavoyle
60	Dundalk	137	Stromboli	162	Ballyroney
61	Sligo	138	Volcano	163	Banbridge
62	Tyrone	139	Etna	164	Fintona
				165	Newbliss

Many of the above, particularly the older classes, were scrapped during the 1950's, some of them earlier. Those remaining in 1959 were divided between the C.I.E. and U.T.A., but none was taken into the permanent stock of the latter.

Nos. 31, 79 and 149 were sold to the S.L. & N.C.R.

2-4-2T's

These were amongst the few passenger tank engines named by the G.N.R. They were built between 1895 and 1902.

90	Aster	14/92	Viola	94	Howth
13/91	Tulip	93	Sutton	95	Crocus

No. 93 has been preserved at Belfast, but not with its name or original green livery.

There was however in addition a series of 4-4-0T's, some of which bore names (all scrapped 1920/1).

7	Ardee
96	Windsor
97	Lisburn

There were also two odd engines.

203	Kells	0-4-0ST
204	Mullingar	0-6-0T

These were scrapped in 1930 by which time they had already been de-named.

Older G.N.R. engines of the century which were all scrapped before the First World War were as follows. (These all originally built for the Ulster Railway.)

2-2-2

111A   North Star (scrapped 1901)

0-4-2

104A	Owenreagh	111	Carntual
105	Typhoon	112	Donard
106	Tornado	131A	Ovoca
107	Cyclone	132A	Foyle
108	Sirocco	104	Tempest
109	Shannon	78A	Simoom
110	Liffey		

(All scrapped 1906–1912)

2-4-0

112A	Jupiter	123	Tyrone
113	Lucifer	126	Ulster
114A	Lagan	127	Munster
120A	Ulidion	128	Leinster
121A	Dalriada	129	Connaught

(All scrapped 1906–1914)

Belfast and Northern Counties Railway

The old B.N.C.R., which was eventually absorbed by the Midland Railway (Northern Counties Committee), had only a few named engines.

4-4-0 2 CYLINDER COMPOUNDS WITH 7′ 0″ DRIVING WHEELS, BUILT 1895

50   Jubilee.
55   Parkmount.

'Jubilee' was later converted to a simple and was scrapped in 1946. 'Parkmount' remained as a compound until withdrawal in 1945.

2-4-0 2-CYLINDER COMPOUND

57   Galgorm Castle

This engine was scrapped in 1938.

4-4-0 2-CYLINDER COMPOUNDS 6' 0" WHEELS, BUILT 1901/2

3/33 King Edward VII/Binevenagh
34 Queen Alexandra/Knocklayd

They were later rebuilt as simples, when they were renamed as shown. Both went in 1950.

In 1930, by which time the line had come under L.M.S. auspices, a policy of naming all of the 4-4-0's was decided upon, although the scheme was never quite completed. The history of the engines involved is somewhat complicated: some had been rebuilt from 2-cylinder compounds of either 2-4-0 or 4-4-0 type, and some renumbering was also included. The complete scheme may be summarised as follows, but the names shown in brackets were never actually carried by the engines.

1	Glenshesk	67/85	Slieve Gallion
2	Glendun	68	Slieve Bane
3	Glenaan	70	(Portmuck Castle)
4/4a	Glenariff	71	Glenarm Castle
21	County Down	72	(Shane's Castle)
24	County Londonderry	73	(Carn Castle)
28	County Tyrone	74	Dunluce Castle
58	(Lurigethan)	75	Antrim Castle
59/86	(Craiggore)	76	Olderfleet Castle
60	County Donegal	77	(Ballygalley Castle)
61	County Antrim	78	Chichester Castle
62	Slemish	79	Kenbaan Castle
63/87	(Ben Bradagh)/	80	Dunseverick Castle
	Queen Alexandra	81	Carrickfergus Castle
64	Trostan	82	Dunananie Castle
65	Knockagh	83	Carra Castle
66	Ben Madigan	84	Lisanoure Castle

The last survivor, No. 74 'Dunluce Castle,' was withdrawn in 1961 and is now preserved.

N.C.C. 2-6-0's BUILT 1933–1942

90	Duke of Abercorn	97	Earl of Ulster
91	The Bush	98	King Edward VIII
92	The Bann	99	King George VI
93	The Foyle	100	Queen Elizabeth
94	The Maine	101	Lord Masserene
95	The Braid	103	Thomas Somerset
96	Silver Jubilee		

Two others of this class, Nos. 102 and 104, did not receive names. Nos. 90–93 were originally intended to have been 'Earl of Ulster,' 'Sorley Boy,' 'Richard de Burgh' and 'John de Courcy' respectively.

All of these engines are now withdrawn.

Ballycastle Railway

This narrow gauge line was taken over by the N.C.C. in 1924. The three original engines were 0-6-0ST's built in 1879.

    1   Dalriada
    2   Countess of Antrim
    3   Lady Boyd

The last mentioned was scrapped in 1909 and the other two in 1924.

Giant's Causeway Portrush and Bush Valley

This narrow gauge line, electrified in 1899, but retaining part steam working, had two named engines.

    3   Dunluce Castle
    4   Brian Boroimhe

They were sold in 1930 to a firm of contractors and remained at work for a few years afterwards.

County Donegal Railways Joint Committee

This narrow gauge line, jointly owned by the Great Northern of Ireland and the Midland Railway of England, named all of its steam locomotives:—

			Built	*Withdrawn*
1	Alice	2-4-0T	1881	1926
2	Blanche	2-4-0T	1881	1912
3	Lydia	2-4-0T	1881	1912
21/1	Ballyshannon/Alice	2-6-4T	1912	
2a/2	Strabane/Blanche	2-6-4T	1912	
3a/3	Stranorlar/Lydia	2-6-4T	1912	
4	Meenglas	4-6-0T	1893	1935
5	Drumboe	4-6-0T	1893	1931
6	Inver	4-6-0T	1893	1931
7	Finn	4-6-0T	1893	1931
8	Foyle	4-6-0T	1893	1935
9	Columbkille	4-6-0T	1893	1935
10	Sir James	4-4-4T	1901	1933
11	Hercules	4-4-4T	1901	1933
12/9	Eske	4-6-4T	1904	1954
13/10	Owenea	4-6-4T	1904	1953
14/11	Erne	4-6-4T	1904	
15/12	Mourne	4-6-4T	1904	1953
16/4	Donegal/Meenglas	2-6-4T	1907	
17/5	Glenties/Drumboe	2-6-4T	1907	
18/6	Killybegs/Columbkille	2-6-4T	1907	
19	Letterkenny	2-6-4T	1907	1940
20/8	Foyle	2-6-4T	1907	

'Letterkenny' was to have been No. 7 'Finn' but was scrapped before the change could be effected.

The remaining engines were all in existence when the line was closed in 1959 and some of them have been sent to the U.S.A.

There was also a 0-4-0 Diesel engine originally built for the Clogher Valley in 1929 as a steam shunter.

No. 11 Phoenix

This loco has been preserved.

Londonderry and Lough Swilly Railway

The L. & L.S.R., the largest narrow-gauge system in the British Isles (the distance from Londonderry to Burtonport alone was 74½ miles), did not name its locomotives since its earlier days, but there were a few exceptions.

One of the original 3′ 0″ gauge 0-6-0T's survived until comparatively recently, this was the old No. 4, name 'Innishowen'. It latterly became No. 17 and lost its name about 1928, but remained in existence until 1940, when it was scrapped.

There were also three 4-6-2T's, built in 1901, and 1904, which bore names for a time, although they were latterly removed.

		Scrapped
7	King Edward VII	1940
9	Aberfoyle	1938
10	Richmond	1954

Clogher Valley Railway

This narrow gauge steam tramway line, closed in 1942, possessed six 0-4-2T's, built 1886/7 and a 0-4-4T (No. 7), built in 1910.

1	Caledon	5	Colebrooke
2	Errigal	6	Erne
3	Blackwater	7	Blessingbourne
4	Fury		

Castlederg and Victoria Bridge

Another roadside tramway, closed in 1933.

The two original tram engines, Nos. 1 and 2, were named 'Mourne' and 'Derg' and there was also a later engine, No. 5, a 0-4-4T, built in 1912, named 'Castlederg', as depicted on the maker's photograph, but it is doubtful whether it ever carried it in service.

Sligo Leitrim and Northern Counties Railway

This railway was somewhat unique in that it never numbered its loco-motives. The names were carried on large handsome brass plates on the tank sides, or in the case of the few tender engines, on smaller ones on the splashers.

The locomotive stock may be summarised as follows:—

		Built	Scrapped
Pioneer	0-6-2T	1877	1928
Sligo	,,	1877	1928
Waterford	0-6-0T	1893	1928
Blacklion	4-4-0	1885	1937
	Purchased 1931 from G.N.R.		
Glencar	4-4-0	1887	1928
	Purchased 1931 from G.N.R.		
Glencar	0-6-0	1890	1950
	Purchased 1928 from G.N.R.		
Sligo	0-6-0	1890	1941*
	Purchased 1931 from G.N.R.		
Sligo	0-6-0	1882	1950
	Purchased 1940 from G.N.R.		

* This engine was returned to the G.N.R. in 1940 in exchange for the third 'Sligo'. These three 0-6-0's had been G.N.R. 31, 149 and 69. The two 4-4-0's were former G.N.R. 118 and 119. Further reference to these locomotives will be found under the G.N.R. heading.

The principal classes of locomotive in use on the S.L. & N.C.R. were all of the 0-6-4T type, of which there were two main varieties, five small ones of considerably ancient appearance and five of a more modern variety.

	Built	Scrapped		Built	Scrapped
Leitrim	1882	1952	Sir Henry	1904	1957
Fermanagh	1882	1952	Enniskillen	1905	1957
Lurganboy	1895	1953	Lough Gill	1915	1957
Lissadell	1899	1957	Lough Melvin	1949	
Hazlewood	1899	1957	Lough Erne	1949	

The final two engines are notable as being the last new steam locomotives to be constructed for any Irish railway. On the closure of the line they were transferred to the U.T.A. as Nos. 26 and 27, still retaining their names. They were still in service in 1966.

Dundalk Newry and Greenore Railway

This Irish offshoot of the L.N.W.R. had six 0-6-0ST's of Crewe design, built between 1873 and 1898.

All carried names on the saddle tanks, not of standard L.N.W.R. lettering although the number plates were in fact so.

1	Macrory	3	Dundalk	5	Carlingford
2	Greenore	4	Newry	6	Holyhead

The line was later taken over by the G.N.R. but the engines were never renumbered. No. 5 had been scrapped in 1929, but the others remained in existence until the final closure of the line in 1951, although some of them had been out of service for a considerable time.

VII

Independent and Miscellaneous

In the following pages are summarised the remaining railways which possessed named engines in England, Wales and Scotland, which did not come within the sphere of any of the four groups at the 1923 amalgamation. A number of them come under the category of light railways and most of these were at one time passenger carrying lines, although the majority are now closed. A few industrial concerns are also included, but it would not be practicable to list all such lines in their entirety. This would take a volume in itself, and it is only possible to give brief details of a few of particular interest, especially from the point of view of the names borne by the locomotives.

Ashover Light Railway

1' 11½" gauge

Bridget	4-6-0T ex W.D. (U.S.A. type built by Baldwins)
Georgie	,, ,, ,, ,, ,, ,, ,,
Guy	,, ,, ,, ,, ,, ,, ,,
Hummie	,, ,, ,, ,, ,, ,, ,,
Joan	,, ,, ,, ,, ,, ,, ,,
Peggy	,, ,, ,, ,, ,, ,, ,,

Passenger service ceased 1937. Closed to all traffic 1950.

Baddesley Collieries, Atherstone

John Roberts	0-6-0ST	Manning Wardle	1916
William Stratford	0-6-0T	Barclay	1923
William Francis	0-4-4-0 Garratt	Beyer Peacock	1937

'William Francis' is the last surviving Garratt engine in the country.

Bideford, Westward Ho! and Appledore Railway

1	Grenville	2-4-2T	Hunslet	1896
2	Kingsley	,,	,,	,,
3	Torridge	,,	,,	,,

Line closed 1917.

Bishops Castle Railway

| Bishops Castle | 2-4-0 | George England | 1861 | Scrapped 1905 |
| Carlisle | 0-6-0 | Kitson | 1867 | |

Carlisle was scrapped when the line was closed in 1936.

Bluebell Railway

27	Primrose	S.E. & C.R.	0-6-0T	Ashford	1910	Late B.R.	31027
323	Bluebell	„	„	„	„	„	„	31323
55	Stepney	L.B. & S.C.R.	„	Brighton	1875	„	„	32655
473	Birch Grove	„	„	„	1898	„	„	32473
72	Fenchurch	„	„	„	1872	„	„	32636

These engines were acquired from B.R. during 1960–1964. 'Primrose' has recently been restored to S.E.&C.R. livery and been de-named accordingly.

Bowater's Paper Mills, Sittingbourne

| Standard gauge | Jubilee | 0-4-0ST | Bagnall | |
| | Pioneer II | 0-6-0T | late S.R. 31178 Ashford 1910 | |

The latter engine is turned out in a style approximating to the old S. E. & C.R. livery with name painted on the tank sides.

2' 6" gauge	Premier	0-4-2ST	Kerr Stuart		1904
	Leader	„	„	„	1906
	Excelsior	„	„	„	1908
	Chevalier	0-6-2T	Manning Wardle		1915
	Superior	„	Kerr Stuart		1920
	Conqueror	„	Bagnall		1922
	Unique	2-4-0T fireless	„		1923
	Melior	0-4-2ST	Kerr Stuart		1924
	Victor	0-4-0T fireless	Bagnall		1929
	Alpha	0-6-2T	„		1932
	Triumph	„	„		1934
	Superb	„	„		1940
	Monarch	0-4-4-0T	„		1953

All still in active service, 1962. These engines carry cast nameplates on the tank sides and are kept in immaculate condition. This is one of the few remaining narrow gauge industrial systems still in operation, with a long 'main line', about three miles in length, with a number of trains daily conveying wood pulp from the docks at Ridham to the paper mills, and in addition several somewhat primitive workmen's trains for the convenience of the employees.

The 0-4-4-0T Monarch has recently been acquired by the Welshpool & Llanfair Preservation Society.

Brampton Railway

Tichborne/Belted Will	0-6-0T	Stephenson	1872
Dandie Dinmont	0-4-0T	Neilson	1881
Sheriff	0-6-0ST	Barclay	1900 sold 1908
Naworth	0-4-0ST	,,	1914
Stephenson	0-6-0ST	,,	1926 ⎫ Colliery
Tindale	,,	,,	,, ⎭ branch

The line was closed in 1923, except for a short colliery branch, and the engines scrapped or sold. It is interesting to recall that Stephenson's 'Rocket', now in South Kensington Museum, worked on the line between 1837 and 1851.

Campbeltown and Machrihanish Light Railway

2′ 3″ gauge

Chevalier	0-4-2ST	Barclay	1883
Princess	,,	Kerr Stuart	1900
Argyll	0-6-2T	Barclay	1906
Atlantic	,,	,,	1907

Closed 1931 and engines broken up.

Cannock Chase and Wolverhampton Railway

McClean	0-4-2ST	Beyer Peacock		1856	Scrapped 1956	
Alfred Paget	,,	,,	,,	1861	,,	1950
Chawner	,,	,,	,,	1864	,,	1949
Brown	,,	,,	,,	1867	,,	1926
Anglesey	,,	,,	,,	1872	,,	1947
Griffin	0-6-0ST	Kitsons		1913		
Foggo	0-4-2ST	Chasetown		1946		

It will be noted that the original 'McClean' was exactly 100 years old when scrapped, and although it had not been in service for two or three years was then the oldest working locomotive in the country.

'Foggo' built in 1946 from parts supplied from Beyer Peacock was substantially the same 90 year old design.

Cannock and Rugeley Colliery

1	Marquis	0-6-0ST	Lilleshall	1867
2	Anglesey	,,	,,	1868
3	Progress	,,	Peckett	1899
4	Rawnsley	,,	Lilleshall	1872
5	Beaudesert	,,	Fox Waller	1879

6	Adjutant	„	Manning Wardle	1917	
7	Birch	2-4-0T	Rawnsley	1888	Scrapped 1956
7	Wimblebury	0-6-0ST	Hunslet	1956	
8	Harrison	0-6-0T	Yorkshire Engine Co.	1872	

8 Harrison   0-6-0T   Yorkshire Engine Co. 1872

formerly 2-4-0T purchased from East and West Jn. Railway

9 Cannock Wood   0-6-0T   Brighton   1877

formerly L.B. & S.C.R. No. 110 (see page 114).

City and South London Railway

This line, the first of London's tube railways, opened in 1890, was worked by electric locomotives until 1922.

One of them, No. 10, bore the name 'Princess of Wales'.

Corringham Light Railway

'Kynite'   0-4-2T   Kerr Stuart   1900

Line closed 1947.

Dorking Greystone Lime Company

Standard gauge.

3	Baxter	0-4-0T	Fletcher Jennings	1877

3' 2" gauge.

4	Townsend Hook	0-4-0T	Fletcher Jennings	1880
5	William Finlay	0-4-0T	„	„

The narrow gauge system was closed in 1957, and the standard in 1960. Both of the narrow gauge locos are preserved into private ownership, and No. 3 has been acquired by the Bluebell Railway as a museum piece.

Duffield Bank Railway

15" gauge

Effie	0-4-0T	built 1874
Ella	0-6-0T	„ 1881
Muriel	0-8-0T	„ 1894

The line was closed in 1916, the last two engines going to the Ravenglass and Eskdale Railway.

Easingwold Railway

Easingwold	0-6-0ST	Hudswell Clark	1891	Sold 1903
Easingwold No. 2	„	„	„	1903	Scrapped 1949

East Kent Light Railway

Walton Park   0-6-0ST   Hudswell Clark 1908   Sold 1943

There was also a 0-6-0ST built by Hawthorn Leslie in 1912, which was lettered and named East Kent Railway 'Gabrielle', but there is no evidence that it ever ran on that railway. No other engines on this line bore names.

Eastwell Quarries, Waltham-on-the-Wold

Metre gauge

Name	Type	Builder	Year	Notes
The Baronet	0-4-0ST	Markham	1889	Transferred from Cranford Ironstone Co.
		Withdrawn 1949, scrapped 1960		
Dreadnought	0-4-2ST	Manning Wardle	1910	Scrapped 1960
54 Nantes	0-6-0T	Louvet (France)	1903	Scrapped 1960
Cambrai	0-6-0T	Corfet (France)	1888	Transferred from Loddington Quarries 1956.

The line was closed 1958. The last two engines were among the very few French built locomotives ever to run in Great Britain. 'Cambrai' is preserved at the Tal-y-Llyn Railway museum, Towyn.

Edge Hill Light Railway

Sankey   0-4-0ST   Manning Wardle 1888

There were also two L.B. & S.C.R. 'Terriers', originally 73 and 74 (see page 112) but they bore no names on the E.H.L.R. The line was closed in 1925, but the engines lay derelict at Kineton until 1946, when they were broken up.

Festiniog Railway

Gauge 1' 11½"

No.	Name	Type	Builder	Year	Notes
1	Princess	0-4-0ST	George England	1863	Withdrawn 1946
2	Prince	„	„	„	„
4	Palmerston	0-4-0ST	„	„	„ Scrapped 1955
5	Welsh Pony	„	„	„	1867 Withdrawn 1938
6	Little Giant	„	„	„	1867 Scrapped 1936
8	James Spooner	0-4-4-0T	Avonside	1872	Scrapped 1933
9	Taliesin	0-4-4T	Vulcan	1876	Scrapped 1935
10	Merddyn Emrys	0-4-4-0T	Boston Lodge	1879	
11/3	Livingstone Thompson/Taliesin/Earl of Merioneth*	0-4-4-0T	Boston Lodge	1885	
11	Moelwyn	2-4-0	diesel Baldwin	1917	
—	Linda	0-4-0ST	Hunslet	1893	⎱ Acquired from
—	Blanche	„	„	„	⎰ Penrhyn Rly.

(See page 167)

*On one side of the engine the name is displayed in its Welsh version, Iarll Meirionydd.

The line was closed in 1946, reopened 1955 under the auspices of the Festiniog Railway Society.

Furzebrook Railway, Wareham

2' 8" gauge.

Primus	0-4-2T	Belliss and Seekings	1866	Scrapped 1900
Secundus	0-6-0WT	„ „	1872	Preserved in Birmingham Science Museum
Tertius	0-6-0ST	Manning Wardle	1886	
Quartus	0-4-2T	J. Fowler	1880	Scrapped 1934
Quintus	0-4-0ST	Manning Wardle	1914	Scrapped 1957
Sextus	0-4-2ST	Peckett	1925	Scrapped 1957
Septimus	0-4-2ST	Peckett	1930	

Line closed 1957.

Glyn Valley Tramway

2' 4½" gauge

Dennis	0-4-2T	Beyer Peacock		1888
Sir Theodore	0-4-2T	„ „		1888
Glyn	0-4-2T	„ „		1892

Line closed 1936.

Groudle Glen Railway

Isle of Man 2' 0" gauge.

Sea Lion	2-4-0T	Bagnall	1898
Polar Bear	2-4-0T	Bagnall	1908

Line disused 1940–1949, later reopened, but since again closed.

Irthlingboro' Ironworks, Northants
(Ebbw Vale Steel, Iron & Coal Co.)

Stephenson	0-6-0ST	R. Stephenson	1896

Originally Port Talbot Railway No. 1 later Ebbw Vale No. 22 Scrapped 1959.

Isle of Man Railway

3' 6" gauge.

1	Sutherland	2-4-0T	Beyer Peacock		1873
2	Derby	„	„	„	1873
3	Pender	„	„	„	1873
4	Loch	„	„	„	1874

5	Mona	2-4-0T	Beyer Peacock	1874
6	Peveril	,,	,, ,,	1875
7	Tynwald	,,	,, ,,	1880
8	Fenella	,,	,, ,,	1894
9	Douglas	,,	,, ,,	1896
10	G. H. Wood	,,	,, ,,	1905
11	Maitland	,,	,, ,,	1905
12	Hutchinson	,,	,, ,,	1908
13	Kissack	,,	,, ,,	1910
14	Thornhill	,,	,, ,,	1880
15	Caledonia	0-6-0T	Dübs & Co.	1885
16	Mannin	2-4-0T	Beyer Peacock	1926

Nos. 14 and 15 were formerly Manx Northern engines (see page 163). All still in existence in 1962, although some have not been used for some years. The line ceased operation in 1965.

Jersey Railway

3' 6" gauge.

1	St. Helier's	2-4-0T	Manning Wardle	1884
2	St. Aubin's	,,	,, ,,	1884
3	Corbiere	,,	W. Bagnall	1893
4	St. Brelade's	,,	,,	1895
5	La Moye	,,	A. Barclay	1907
1	The Pioneer	Steam railcar	Sentinel	1923
2	Portelet	,,	,, ,,	1924
3	La Moye	,,	,, ,,	1924
4	Normandie	,,	,, ,,	1925

Line closed 1936.

Jersey Eastern Railway

Standard gauge

	Caesarea	0-4-2T	Kitson	1872
	Calvados	,,	,,	1872
	Mont Orgueil	,,	,,	1886
	Cartaret	,,	,,	1898
	North Western	0-4-0T	Sharp Stewart	1870
	Normandie	Steam railcar	Sentinel	1925
	Brittany	,,	,,	1927

Line closed 1929, when railcar 'Normandie' was transferred to the Jersey Railway (see above) and the engine part of 'Brittany' came to England to work in the Merstham Lime Quarries, Surrey.

Penrhyn
Railway—
'Nesta'.

Penrhyn Railway—Nameplate of
'Jubilee' 1897.

[*L.P.C.*

One of the three 'main line' engines of the Penrhyn Railway. 'Charles' is now preserved in
Carnarvon Museum, but his two sisters 'Blanche' and 'Linda' continue to lead an active life on
the Festiniog Railway.

Leiston Engineering Works 'Sirapite' was one of the last Aveling and Porter engines to remain
at work.

Longmoor Military Railway. Former Taff Vale engine 'Gordon'.

Longmoor Military Railway—nameplate on former North Stafford engine.

Lancashire Collieries, former North Stafford engine 'Princess'.

[*R. M. Casserley*
Bowater's Paper Mills, Sittingbourne 'Pioneer II', formerly a S.E. & C.R. engine.

[*R. M. Casserley*
'Stephenson' started life as Port Talbot Railway No. 1. It was subsequently sold to the Ebbw Vale Iron and Steel Co., who latterly used it at their iron ore works at Irthlingboro', Northants. It was scrapped in 1959.

South Hetton Colliery 0-6-0ST 'Sir George', a very ancient engine with an interesting history. Originally built as a tender engine in 1848 for the L.N.W.R., it was converted to saddle tank in 1866. Sold to Alexandra Docks Railway in 1875, and again to the South Hetton Colliery in 1898, where it worked until scrapped in 1953. The date '1911' on the number plate is a rebuilding date.

Port of London
Authority—No. 23
'Jason'.

Baddesley Collieries 'William Francis'. The last remaining Garratt engine in this country.

[R. M. Casser.

Rothervale Collieries—'Rothervale No. 0'.

Kent and East Sussex Railway

(formerly Rother Valley Rly.)

1	Tenterden	2-4-0T	Hawthorn Leslie	1899	Scrapped 1941
2	Northiam	„	„ „	1899	„ 1941
3	Bodiam	0-6-0T	Brighton	1872	
4	Hecate	0-8-0T	Hawthorn Leslie	1904	Sold to S.R. 1932
5	Rolvenden	0-6-0T	Brighton	1872	Scrapped 1938
7	Rother	0-6-0	Beyer Peacock	1873	„ 1938
8	Hesperus	0-6-0ST	Manning Wardle	1876	„ 1941
9	Juno	0-6-0	Beyer Peacock	1873	„ 1938

On Nationalisation in 1948 the surviving engine No. 3 (which had previously lost its name) came back into S.R. stock as No. 32670. It had originally been L.B. & S.C.R. 70 (see page 112). It was still running in 1962. The other 'Terrier', No. 5, was formerly L.B. & S.C.R. No. 671 (originally 71). 'Hecate' became S.R. 949 and was scrapped as such in 1950, retaining its name until the end. Part of this line is being reopened by a preservation society, and amongst other engines acquired is the original No. 3, 'Bodiam'.

Leiston Engineering Works, Leiston, Suffolk

This works possesses only one engine, but it is of unusual interest in being almost the only remaining Aveling and Porter geared locomotive still at work in this country.

Sirapite   Aveling and Porter   1906   Acquired from Gypsum mines, Mountfield

Lincolnshire Coast Light Railway, Cleethorpes

1' 11½" gauge

This short line, newly opened as recently as 1960, possesses three engines.

					Origin
Jurassic	0-6-0ST	Peckett	1903	Rugby Cement Co. (See page 169)
Elin	0-4-0ST	Hunslet	1899	Penrhyn (See page 166)
Peter	„	Bagnall	1917	Cliff Hill Granite Co.

Longmoor Military Railway

1st W.D. No.	Later W.D. No.	Name	Type	Builder	Date	Notes
		Kingsley	4-4-0T	Hudswell Clarke	1880	Late M.&G.N.R.J. No. 10. Name latterly removed. Scrapped since 1946

M

1st W.D. No.	Later W.D. No.	Name	Type	Builder	Date	Notes
		Longmoor	0-4-4T	Swindon	1890	Late G.W.R. No. 34. Scrapped 1921
70205		Gordon	0-6-2T	Cardiff	1897	Late G.W.R. 450. Originally Taff Vale Rly. Sold 1947. Recently acquired for preservation
		Kitchener/ Wellington	0-6-2T	Kitson	1886	Late G.W.R. 579. Originally Taff Vale. Scrapped 1944
70206		Earl Roberts	2-4-2T	Crewe	1891	Late L.M.S. 6610. Originally L.N.W.R. Scrapped 1945
		Earl Haig	2-4-2T	Crewe	1891	Late L.M.S. 6613. Originally L.N.W.R. Scrapped 1946
70203		Sir John French	0-6-2T	H. Leslie	1914	Scrapped 1946
70204		Selbourne	0-6-0T	„	1922	Sold 1947
70207		Marlborough*	0-6-2T	Stoke 1909	1909	Late L.M.S. 2253. Originally N.S.R. Sold 1947
70208		Kitchener	0-6-2T	Bagnall	1938	Sold 1948
72400		Earl Roberts	4-4-2T	Brighton	1908	Late S.R. 2013. Originally L.B. & S.C.R. Scrapped 1949
70271	876	Bari	0-6-0	Diesel Electric Derby	1945	
70272	878	Chittagong	0-6-0	„	1945	

* This engine also carried a plaque beneath the nameplate itself bearing the inscription: 'Designed by John R. Adams. Built at Stoke works 1909 for North Staffordshire Rly. Classification New L No. 158. Taken over by L.M.S. 1923. Purchased by War Dept. 1936'.

1st	Later	Name	Type	Builder	Date
71232	890	Tobruk	0-4-4O Diesel Electric	Whitecomb	194
71233	891	Algiers	0-4-4O Diesel Electric	,,	1941
72214	807	Caen	0-4-0 Diesel	Ruston & Hornsby	1945
72220	829	Basra	0-4-0	Drewry	1945
71443	157	Constantine	0-6-0ST	Hunslet	1945
71505	118	Brussels	0-6-0ST	Hudswell Clarke	1945
75028	100	Ahwaz	0-6-0ST	Hunslet	1943
75040	106	Spyck	0-6-0ST	,,	1943
75041	107	Foggia	0-6-0ST	,,	1943
75042	108	Jullundur	0-6-0ST	,,	1943
75079	114	Sir John French/ Lisieux	0-6-0ST	Robert Stephenson & Hawthorn	1943
75189	152	Rennes	0-6-0ST	,,	1944
75275	177	Matruh	0-6-0ST	,,	1945
75277	178	Foligno	0-6-0ST	,,	1945
75282	181	Insein	0-6-0ST	Vulcan Foundry	1945
75290	186	Manipur Road	0-6-0ST	,,	1945
73797	601	The Sapper/ Kitchener	2-10-0	N.B. Loco Co.	1945
77337	400	Sir Guy William/ La Deliverance	2-8-0	,,	1943
79250	401	Major General McMullen	2-8-0	Vulcan Foundry	1945
93257	700	Major General Carl R. Gray, Jr.	2-8-0	Alco (U.S.A.)	1944
94382	300	Major General Frank S. Ross	0-6-0T	Davenport (U.S.A.)	1943

The first series of numbers was allocated by the War Department about 1945, previously the engines had been un-numbered.

Manx Northern Railway

3' 0" gauge

1	Ramsey	2-4-0T	Sharp Stewart	1879	Scrapped 1918
2	Northern	2-4-0T	,,	1879	,, 1912
3	Thornhill	2-4-0T	Beyer Peacock	1880	
4	Caledonia	0-6-0T	Dübs & Co.	1885	

Nos. 3 and 4 became Isle of Man Railway 14 and 15 in 1905 (see page 160).

Mersey Railway

1	The Major	0-6-4T	Beyer Peacock	1885
2	Earl of Chester	0-6-4T	„	1885
3	Duke of Lancaster	0-6-4T	„	1885
4	Gladstone	0-6-4T	„	1885
5	Cecil Raikes	0-6-4T	„	1886
6	Fox	0-6-4T	„	1886
7	Liverpool	0-6-4T	„	1886
8	Birkenhead	0-6-4T	„	1886
9	Connaught	0-6-4T	„	1886
10	Mersey	2-6-2T	„	1887
11	Victoria	2-6-2T	„	1887
12	Bouverie	2-6-2T	„	1887
13	Brunlees	2-6-2T	„	1887
14	Tranmere	2-6-2T	„	1887
15	Salisbury	2-6-2T	„	1892
16	Burcot	2-6-2T	„	1892
17	Burnley	2-6-2T	„	1892
18	Banstead	2-6-2T	„	1892

When the line was electrified in 1903 the engines were sold out of service. Some went to Australia, and it was reported that at least one of them was working quite recently. Nos. 5 and 8 were sold to the Shipley Collieries, Derbyshire, where 'Cecil Raikes' was at work until 1954, since when it has been stored at Derby pending being restored for preservation.

Nidd Valley Light Railway

1 Holdsworth	4-4-0T	Beyer Peacock	1871	Purchased from Met. District Railway
2 Milner	„	„ „	1879	Purchased from Met. District Railway
Milner	0-6-0T	Hudswell Clarke	1909	
Hill	Steam railcar	Kerr Stuart	1905	Purchased from G.W.R. (No. 16)
Haig	0-6-0ST	Manning Wardle	1890	
Allenby	„	„ „	1889	
Beattie	„	„ „	1905	
Kitchener	„	Peckett	1902	
Ian Hamilton	„	Hudswell Clarke	1898	
Mitchell	„	„ „	1916	
Watson	„	„ „	1916	
Craven	0-4-0ST	„ „	1920	
Blythe	0-6-0ST	Avonside	1922	
Gadie	„	A. Barclay	1925	
Trotter	0-4-0ST	„	„	
Stringer	„	„	„	

The line was closed during the 1930's and the remaining engines scrapped or sold.

North Sunderland Railway

Bamburgh	0-6-0ST	Manning Wardle	1878	Scrapped 1949
The Lady Armstrong	Diesel	A. Whitworth	1933	Sold 1949

Latterly until 1951, when the line was closed altogether, an engine was hired from the N.E.R.

Padarn Railway (Dinorwic Quarries)

Main line 4′ 0″ gauge.

Jenny Lind	0-4-0	A. Horlock, Northfleet Iron-works.	1848	Scrapped 1886
Fire Queen	„	A. Horlock, Northfleet Iron-works. Preserved at Llanberis	1848	Withdrawn 1886
Dinorwic	0-6-0T	Hunslet	1882	
Amalthea	„	„	1886	
Velinheli	„	„	1895	

The main line of the system, extending for seven miles from the quarries at Llanberis to Port Dinorwic, was closed in 1961 and replaced by road transport. A small part of the extensive 1′ 10¾″ gauge system in the quarries remains open and is worked by a few survivors of the former locomotive stud of 0-4-0ST's bearing the following fascinating series of names:—

Charlie	Hunslet	1870
George	„	1877
Velinheli	„	1886
Alice/King of the Scarlets	„	1889
Enid/Red Damsel	„	1889
Rough Pup	„	1891
Cloister	„	1891
Vaenol/Jerry M.	„	1895
Lady Madcap	„	1898
Port Dinorwic/Cackler	„	1898
Wellington/Bernstein	„	1898
Covert Coat	„	1898
George B.	„	1898
Holy War	„	1902
Alice	„	1902
Maid Marian	„	1903
Irish Mail	„	1903
Wild Aster	„	1904
Lady Joan	„	1922
Dolbadarn	„	1922

Michael	„	1932
Sybil	Bagnall	1906
Elidir	Avonside	1933

A few of the above were still in service in 1966. Some have been acquired privately for preservation.

Penrhyn Railway (Penrhyn Quarries)

1′ 11½″ gauge.

Lord Penrhyn	0-4-0 Vertical Boiler	De Winton	1876
Lady Penrhyn	„	„ „	„
Alice	„	„ „	„
Georgina	„	„ „	„
Ina	„	„ „	1877
Kathleen	„	„ „	„
George Henry	„	„ „	„
George Sholto	0-4-0T	Beaston, Derby	1876
Edward Sholto	„	De Winton	1876
Hilda	„	„ „	1877
Violet	„	„ „	„

All of the above were scrapped by 1911 except 'Kathleen' and 'George Henry'. The latter is now preserved in the Tal-y-Llyn museum at Towyn.

Gwynedd	0-4-0ST	Hunslet	1883
Lilian	„	„	„
Winifred	„	„	1885
Lilla	„	„	1891
Margaret	„	„	1894
Alan George	„	„	„
Nesta	„	„	1899
Elin	„	„	„
Hugh Napier	„	„	1904
Pamela	„	„	1906
Sybil Mary	„	„	„
George Sholto	„	„	1909
Edward Sholto	„	„	„
Gertrude	„	„	„
Jubilee 1897	„	Manning Wardle	1897
Sanford	„	Bagnall	1900
Skinner	„	„	1906
Eigiau	0-4-0WT	Orenstein & Koppell	1912
Bronllwyd	0-6-0WT	Hudnall Clarke	1930
Cegin	0-4-0WT	Barclay	1931
Glyder	„	„	„

Ogwen	0-4-0T	Avonside	1933
Marchlyn	"	"	"
Stanhope	0-4-0ST	Kerr Stuart	1917
Sgt. Murphy	0-6-0T	" "	1918
Llandegai	2-6-2T	Baldwins, U.S.A.	1917
Felin Hen	"	" "	"
Tregarth	"	" "	"

All the above are quarry engines. By 1962 only a few were still working, many having been scrapped, and others stored out of service.

For working the main line from the quarries to Port Penrhyn, there were three larger 0-4-0ST's:—

Charles	Hunslet	1882
Blanche	"	1893
Linda	"	"

'Blanche' and 'Linda' have been sold to the Festiniog Railway, whilst 'Charles' is in Carnarvon Museum.

Pentewan Railway

2' 6" gauge.

Pentewan	0-6-0	Manning Wardle	1873
Trewithan	"	" "	1886
Canopus	0-6-2ST	" "	1901
Pioneer	2-6-2T	Yorkshire Engine Co.	1893

The line was closed in 1916.

Port of London Authority

11	Looe	0-6-0ST	Stephenson	1901	Purchased from Liskeard and Caradon Railway
23	Jason	"	Stephenson	1905	late Tilbury & West India Docks Co.
24	Nestor	"	Stephenson	1907	late Tilbury & West India Docks Co.

All now scrapped or sold.

Ravenglass and Eskdale Railway

1' 3" gauge. (formerly 3' 0")

Ella	0-6-0T	Heywood	1881	Formerly Duffield Bank Railway. (see page 157).
Muriel/ River Irt	0-8-0T rebuilt as 0-8-2 tender engine	"	1894	Formerly Duffield Bank Railway. (see page 157).

Sanspareil	4-4-2	Basset Lowke	1912	
Colossus	4-6-2	„ „	1915 ⎫	
Sir Aubrey Brocklebank	4-6-2	Hunt, Bournemouth	1919 ⎬ later combined to form one 4-6-6-4 engine
River Esk	2-8-2	Paxman, Colchester	1923 ⎭	

'River Irt' and 'River Esk' were still in service in 1962. A new 2-8-2, 'River Mite', was built in 1966.

Redruth and Chasewater Railway

Miner	0-6-0ST	Neilson	1854
Smelter	0-4-2ST	„	1854
Spitfire	0-6-0ST	„	1859

All these locomotives were in existence when the line closed in 1915, but by that time 'Smelter' was only occasionally in use.

Romney Hythe and Dymchurch Railway

1′ 3″ gauge

1	Green Goddess	4-6-2	Davey, Paxman	1925
2	Northern Chief	„	„ „	1926
3	Southern Maid	„	„ „	„
4	The Bug	0-4-0	Krauss, Munich	„
5	Hercules	4-8-2	Davey, Paxman	„
6	Samson	„	„ „	„
7	Typhoon	4-6-2	„ „	„
8	Hurricane	„	„ „	„
9	Doctor Syn	„	Yorkshire Engine Co.	1931
10	Black Prince	U.S.A. design	„ „ „	„

No. 4 was sold in 1933.

Rothervale Collieries

This system is included as providing a good example of a method of identification frequently met with in individul concerns. Although not perhaps to be regarded as naming in the strict sense, nevertheless the name of the Company repeated on a succession of engines, followed by No. 1, No. 2, No. 3, etc., on the tank sides, often in the form of a cast plate, may perhaps be regarded as a method of naming not far removed from the well known system adopted on the G.W.R. and other railways. The Rothervale locomotives were particularly interesting in that the numbers commenced at '0' instead of the usual '1', an extremely rare instance of an engine bearing the No. 0, although the method which might be more logically applied in the case of large numbers of units, where the range 0–99, 100–199, etc., would be far more convenient than the alternative but somewhat clumsy system of 1–100, 101–200, etc., which is still sometimes used.

Rothervale No. 0	0-6-0ST	Beyer Peacock	1879
Rothervale No. 1	„	Yorkshire Engine Co.	1929
Rothervale No. 2	„	„ „ „	„
Rothervale No. 3	0-6-0ST	Hudnall Clarke	1891
Rothervale No. 4	„	„ „	„
Rothervale No. 5	„	Hunslet	1944
Rothervale No. 6	„	Hudswell Clarke	1900
Rothervale No. 7	„	Yorkshire Engine Co.	1909
Rothervale No. 8	0-6-0T	Kerr Stuart	1917
Rothervale No. 9	0-6-0ST	Hudswell Clarke	1918
No. 10 Huntsman	„	A. Barclay	1936

The above are the most recently built engines to bear their respective names, earlier members of the family having been scrapped, in some cases for many years. No. 0 itself, which was numbered 1 until 1929, was withdrawn in 1959. Since absorption into the National Coal Board, some of the engines have been dispersed to other collieries in the area.

Rugby Portland Cement Co., Southam

1' 11½" gauge

Jurassic	0-6-0ST	Peckett	1903	
Neozoic	„	„	1906	Scrapped 1943
Liassic	„	„	1909	„ „
Triassic	„	„	1911	
Mesozoic	„	„	1913	
Liassic	„	„	1923	

The system closed in 1957. 'Triassic' is preserved under private ownership the second 'Liassic' went to Canada, and 'Jurassic' now works on the Lincolnshire Coast Light Railway. (See page 161).

Rye and Camber Tramway

3' 0" gauge

1	Camber	2-4-0T	Bagnall	1895
2	Victoria	„	„	1897

Line closed and engines scrapped.

Saundersfoot

4′ 0¾″ gauge

| Rosalind | 0-4-0ST | Manning Wardle | 1874 |
| Bull Dog | „ | Kerr Stuart | 1915 |

Closed 1939 and engines scrapped.

Selsey Tramway

(also known as WEST SUSSEX RAILWAY and Hundred of Manhood and
Selsey Tramway)

1	Selsey	2-4-0T	Peckett	1897	
2	Sidlesham	0-6-0ST	Manning Wardle	1861	Scrapped 1932
3	Hesperus	0-4-2ST	Neilson	1871	Scrapped 1930
4/3	Chichester	0-6-0ST	Hudswell Clarke	1903	Scrapped 1932
4	Morous	„	Manning Wardle	1866	
5	Ringing Rock	„	„	„	1883

Line closed 1935 and remaining engines scrapped. 'Morous' had been
transferred from the Shropshire and Montgomery Railway.

Shropshire and Montgomery Railway

1	Gazelle	0-4-2WT	Dodman, Kings Lynn	1893		
2	Hecate/Severn	0-4-2ST	Bury	1840	Scrapped	1932
3	Hesperus	0-6-0	Beyer Peacock	1875	„	1941
4	Thisbe	0-6-2T	Hawthorn Leslie	1911	Sold	1911
4	Morous	0-6-0ST	Manning Wardle	1866		
5	Pyramus	0-6-2T	Hawthorn Leslie	1911	Sold	1911
5	Pyramus	0-6-0	Beyer Peacock	1874	Scrapped	1932
6	Thisbe	„	„ „	1873	„	„
7	Hecate	0-6-0T	Brighton	1880	„	„
8	Dido	„	„	1878	„	„
9	Daphne	„	„	1880	„	„

The first 4 and 5, new 0-6-2T's were found to be unsuitable for the line and
disposed of soon after delivery. Nos. 3, 5 and 6 were formerly L.S.W.R.
0324, 0300 and 0283. Nos. 7, 8 and 9 were originally L.B. & S.C.R. 'Terriers'
(see page 112) Nos. 81, 38 and 83. No. 1 is preserved by the W.D. at Longmoor,
Hants. No. 4 went to the Selsey Tramway (see above) and scrapped in 1949.
The line closed to passenger traffic in 1933. It was taken over by the W.D.
during the war and finally closed in 1959.

Snowdon Mountain Tramway

2′ 7½″ gauge

The only rack railway in the British Isles.

1	Ladas	0-4-2T	Swiss Loco Works			1895
2	Enid	„	„	„	„	„
3	Wyddfa	„	„	„	„	„
4	Snowdon	„	„	„	„	1896
5	Moel Siabod	„	„	„	„	„
6	Sir Harmood/Padarn	„	„	„	„	1922
7	Eryri/Aylwin	„	„	„	„	1923
8	Eryri	„	„	„	„	„

No. 1 had a very short career, being blown down a ravine during a high wind in 1896 and never recovered. The remainder, with the exception of No. 4, which has been out of service since 1939, were still at work in 1962.

Southwold Railway

3′ 0″ gauge

1	Southwold	2-4-2T	Sharp Stewart		1893
2	Halesworth	2-4-0T	„	„	1897
3	Blyth	„	„	„	„
4	Wenhaston	0-6-2T	Manning Wardle		1916

The line was closed in 1929, when No. 1 was scrapped, but the others remained disused at Southwold until the early 1940's, when they were broken up in the wartime salvage drive.

Surrey Border and Camberley Railway

10½″ gauge

2573	Harvester	4-6-2	built	1934
1003	Western Queen	„		„
2005	Silver Jubilee	„	„	1938
2006	Edward VIII	„	„	1934
2011	Coronation	„	„	1938

Line closed 1940 and engines sold.

Swansea and Mumbles Railway

This tramway, opened as long ago as 1807 with horse traction, and converted to steam working in 1877, was electrified in 1929. At this time, or during the preceding years, there had worked, in addition to the main stock of the company, Nos. 1–5 (unnamed) three 0-6-0T's named 'Swansea', 'Crumlin' and 'Hampshire', although not all at the same time. 'Swansea' and 'Hampshire' were Avonside engines, but the origin of 'Crumlin' is doubtful. All were disposed of by or prior to 1929.

Tal-y-Llyn Railway

2′ 3″ gauge

1	Tal-y-Llyn	0-4-2ST	Fletcher Jennings	1864
2	Dolgoch*	0-4-0WT	„ „	1865
3	Sir Hadyn	0-4-2ST	Falcon	1878
4	Edward Thomas	„	Kerr Stuart	1921
6	Douglas	0-4-0T	Barclay	1918

* Temporarily renamed " Pretoria " about 1900 in commemoration of the Boer War.
Nos. 3 and 4 were originally Corris Railway   (see page 38)

Torrington and Marland Railway

1	Mary	0-6-0ST	Black Hawthorn	1880
2	Marland	0-6-0T	Bagnall	1910
3	Peter	0-4-0T	Lewin	1871
4	Merton	0-4-0	Fletcher Jennings	1875
11	Avonside	0-6-0ST	Avonside	1901
	Jersey No. 1	0-4-0	Fletcher Jennings	1873
	Jersey No. 2	„	„ „	1874

Nos. 1–3 and 11 were scrapped soon after the transfer of the major portion of the line in 1923 to the Southern Railway, who converted it to standard gauge and used it as a part of the North Devon and Cornwall Junction Light Railway. The three old Fletcher Jennings engines became the property of the North Devon Clay Co. and lasted until 1949–1952.

Wantage Tramway

	Raven	0-4-0ST	Avonside	1874	Scrapped 1919
	The Driver	„	Manning Wardle	1875	„ „
5	Shannon	„	George England	1857	

'Raven' was formerly G.W.R. No. 1329 (see page 35). 'Shannon' was built for the Sandy and Potton Railway: it had lost its name by the time it came into the hands of the Wantage Tramway in 1878 and never carried it again during its working life. When the line was finally closed in 1946 however it was taken to Swindon and restored for preservation, the name 'Shannon' being revived on plates on the sides of the boiler barrel. It rested in honourable retirement under a canopy on the platform of Wantage Road station until closed in 1966 when it was removed to premises in Wantage town.

Welsh Highland Railway

1' 11½" gauge

Snowdon Ranger	0-6-4T	Vulcan	1877	Scrapped	1915
Moel Tryfan	„	„		„	1954
Beddgelert	0-6-4ST	Hunslet	„	„	1906
Russell	2-6-2T	„	1906		
Gowrie	0-6-4T	„	1908	Scrapped	1915

The line was closed in 1937. It had been taken over by the Festiniog in 1934, when 'Moel Tryfan' and 'Russell' became Nos. 11 and 12 in the Festiniog stock.

'Russell' was sold in 1941 and after various ownerships finished work at Corfe Castle Clay Mines in Dorset. It is now preserved at the Tal-y-Llyn museum, Towyn.

Welshpool and Llanfair Railway

2' 6" gauge

1	The Earl	0-6-0T	Beyer Peacock	1903
2	The Countess	„	„	„	„
3	Raven	Diesel			
4	Upnor Castle	„			

The original line was taken over by the Cambrian Railway and absorbed by the G.W.R. at the grouping, when the engines became Nos. 822 and 823. The railway was closed in 1956, but has recently been reopened under private auspices, the two steam engines having been stored during the interim period.

Weston, Clevedon and Portishead Railway

1	Clevedon	2-4-0T	Dübs & Co.	1875	Scrapped	1940
2	Portishead	0-6-0ST	Manning Wardle	1890	Sold	1927
2	Portishead	0-6-0T	Brighton	1877		
3	Weston	0-6-0ST	Manning Wardle	1881	Scrapped	1940
4	Hesperus	2-4-0T	Sharp Stewart	1875	„	1937

The line closed in 1940. No. 2 'Portishead' was taken over by the G.W.R. as their No. 5 and was scrapped in 1954. It had originally been L.B. & S.C.R. No. 43 (see page 112).

Whittingham Asylum Railway

1	James Fryars	0-4-2T	Brighton	1886

Originally L.B. & S.C.R. 'Riddlesdown' (later S.R. 2357) purchased 1947 (see page 114).

The line closed in 1957, and the engine scrapped, the last of its class to remain in existence.

Wissington Light Railway

Mac	0-4-0ST	Hudswell Clarke	1899
Cossack	0-6-0ST	Peckett	1898
Newcastle	„	Manning Wardle	1901
Ellesmere	„	Barclay	1909
Hayle	„	Hudswell Clarke	1924
Wissington	„	„　　„	1938

Line closed 1957.

Index of Railways

(See also Appendix, page 178)

Appendix

Remaining passenger carrying railways of the British Isles which had no named engines, and consequently do not figure in these pages:

Barry
Belfast and County Down
Cork and Macroom
Cork Bandon and South Coast
Cork Blackrock and Passage
Furness
Hull and Barnsley
Lancashire Derby and East Coast
Listowel and Ballybunion
Maryport and Carlisle
Metropolitan District
Midland and South Western Junction
Mid Suffolk Light
Neath and Brecon
North London
Port Talbot
Rhondda and Swansea Bay
Somerset and Dorset Joint
South Shields Marsden and Whitburn
Taff Vale
Tralee and Dingle
Waterford and Tramore
Wirral